The Rebel Christ

The Rebel Christ

Michael Coren

Publisher and acquiring editor: Scott Fraser | Editor: Laurie Miller
Cover designer: Laura Boyle | Interior designer: Karen Alexiou

Library and Archives Canada Cataloguing in Publication

Title: The rebel Christ / Michael Coren.
Names: Coren, Michael, author.
Description: Includes bibliographical references.
Identifiers: Canadiana (print) 20210239042 | Canadiana (ebook) 20210239107 | ISBN 9781459748514 (softcover) | ISBN 9781459748521 (PDF) | ISBN 9781459748538 (EPUB)
Subjects: LCSH: Jesus Christ—Person and offices.
Classification: LCC BT203 .C68 2021 | DDC 232—dc23

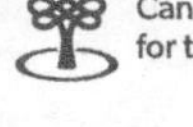

We acknowledge the support of the Canada Council for the Arts and the Ontario Arts Council for our publishing program. We also acknowledge the financial support of the Government of Ontario, through the Ontario Book Publishing Tax Credit and Ontario Creates, and the Government of Canada.

Printed and bound in Canada.

Dundurn Press
1382 Queen Street East
Toronto, Ontario, Canada M4L 1C9
dundurn.com, @dundurnpress

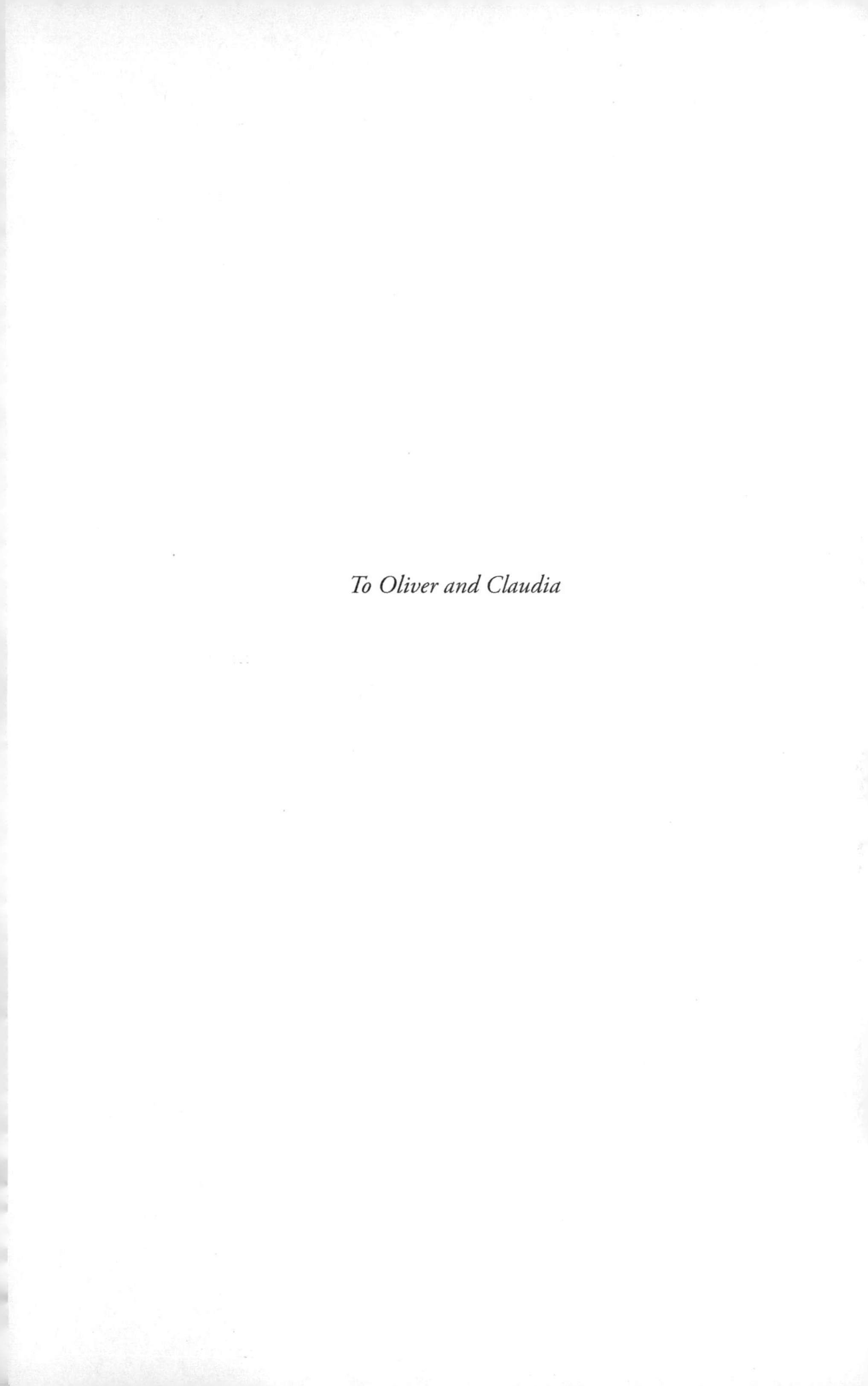

To Oliver and Claudia

Contents

Author's Note ix

Introduction 1

1: Church, Community, the Divide, and the Debate 13

2: Jesus Hates Commies 33

3: God Made People Gay, He Didn't Make Them Gay-Hating 67

4: Life Begins at ... Being Really, Really Angry About Abortion 109

A Last Word 133

Bibliography 147

About the Author 149

Author's Note

Let me say immediately that while I am ordained in the Anglican Church of Canada and have great love and respect for my church, what follows are my own words, and I write and speak only for myself and not in any way for my parish, diocese, bishop, or church. There are, however, so many people within that church who have helped me so much, so often, to understand what it means to be a true follower of the rebel Christ. To those saints, to those friends, to those colleagues, I shall be forever grateful. There are also a number of people who have helped to form and shape me as a Christian, especially in the past eight years since I had something of a conversion, and they come from all denominations and backgrounds. They also come from outside of any church, and some of them aren't Christians at all — we should learn from all people, including those who steadfastly reject organized belief. I can say with confidence that intelligent and generous atheists have often revealed to me what truth and kindness genuinely mean. For all of these people, I shall be forever in your debt, not only because you changed me but also because you enabled me to reach the point where a book such as this was possible. But, of course, none of them are responsible for any faults or failings in what I have written — all of those are down to me alone.

Introduction

The starting point for this book is a question, based on a claim. Why is it that the purest, most supremely liberating philosophy and theology in all of history is now seen by so many people around the world as an intolerant, legalistic, and even irrelevant religion embraced only by the gullible, the foolish, and the judgmental? If that shocks you, so be it. That's a good and not a bad thing, and the truth is often shocking. As a Christian, as someone whose faith informs his entire life and meaning, I pose this question with no relish and with a great deal of remorse, but I pose it nevertheless because it's real and it's proven, and unless Christians admit the problem and struggle to remedy it, matters will only deteriorate. For Christians and for non-Christians alike, for the sake of public discourse, for the sake of the church, and for the sake of generations to come, we have to set matters right.

An authentic relationship with God is a dialogue, and one that involves questions, arguments, and even doubt. We're made — and if we're Christians we believe we're made by God — to be thinking individuals who want answers, and not robotic creatures who simply obey. A mature belief in Scripture necessitates an understanding that the Bible is not divine dictation but an inspired history of God's relationship with humanity, which is a wonderful guide to life but doesn't solve every modern problem and hourly challenge. It can be complex; it's often nuanced; some would argue, although I disagree, that it's even contradictory; but at heart it's about absolute love. And that love culminates in the life, death, and resurrection of Christ, who says not a word about, for example, abortion, homosexuality, euthanasia, pornography, or the so-called traditional family, but demands justice, forgiveness, equality, care for the poor and for the marginalized and for strangers, and compassion even for enemies; who insists on peace, and on the abandonment of materialism; and who constantly speaks of the blistering risks of wealth and prestige.

He turns the world upside down, he challenges the comfortable and the complacent, sides with the outcast and the prisoner, and has no regard for earthly power and worldly ambition. Love and hope. Christianity isn't safe and was never supposed to be. Christianity is dangerous. Yet, truth be told, we have often transformed a faith that should revel in saying yes into a religion that cries no. Its founder died so that we would change the world but many of his followers fight to defend the establishment, they try to link Jesus to nationalism and military force, and they dismiss those who campaign for social change as being radical and even godless.

Of course, this is only a culture within Christianity, and not Christianity itself, but ask most people what they think of when they consider the public face of the Christian faith and they speak of American conservative politicians, anti-abortion activists, or campaigners against sex education or equal marriage. Worse than this, many Christians themselves — especially in North America — have retreated into a bunker mentality, seeing persecution around every corner and retreating into literalism and small-mindedness. They have built an alternative culture, not one that's anchored in the simplicity and altruism of the early church, but that's hinged on nationalism and insularity.

This is all nostalgia rather than the Jesus movement, and as much as change can be frightening to all of us, the Son of God told us that fear and anxiety are unfounded. If we worry about the evolving world, we're just not listening to the words of Christ that we claim to revere. It's as though the cosmetics of the Gospels, the veneer of the message, have become more important than its core and its central meaning. Jesus spoke less about the end times than the time to end injustice, less about whom we should love than about how we should love everyone. If we miss that, we're missing the whole thing. The great C.S. Lewis, one of the finest communicators of the faith in modern times, once wrote that "Christianity, if false, is of no importance, and if true, of infinite importance. The only thing it cannot be is moderately important." Let Christians not be moderate in their vocation as radicals of invincible and, yes, revolutionary love.

I know of what I speak, because this is in many ways a book that has grown from personal experience. Until 2013 I was regarded as a champion of orthodox Roman Catholicism, and as such an opponent of reproductive rights for women, equal marriage, and many other issues around which I now have an extremely different and certainly more qualified opinion. In Canada, I hosted a nightly television show for sixteen years, had a radio show for even longer, and was published in numerous major secular newspapers, as well as several Catholic ones. My book *Why Catholics Are Right* sold almost fifty thousand copies and was on various bestseller lists for eleven weeks. I spoke to large crowds all over North America and in the U.K. I certainly wasn't on the hard right: I supported civil unions and legal protection for LGBTQ2 people, I opposed the Iraq war and the death penalty, I supported the welfare state and the forgiving of Third World debt. But it was these areas of liberalism, these informed subtleties, that made my overall Christian conservatism so persuasive. The fanatics could rant and be ignored; a relatively intelligent and seemingly reasonable commentator far less so. Because of that, and to my shame, I caused much more harm.

That's a little surprising, in that I come from a British, secular, half-Jewish family. It was while I was working on a biography of

G.K. Chesterton, a flawed but brilliant British, Catholic author and journalist who died in 1936, that I became interested in Roman Catholicism, particularly of the more traditional kind, and in 1984 was baptized and confirmed. I found a home among conservatives, and intellectual, emotional, and spiritual love-bombing and praise are difficult to resist. But I have nothing and nobody to blame other than myself. I threw myself into a contrarian defence of Catholic reaction, and to my shame I was rather good at it.

But then in came God, who can be extremely annoying in that way! Genuine faith is sandpaper of the soul. It hurts, it stings, but in the final analysis it should lead to a more perfect believer. I suppose that the divine carpenter began work on me, because around eight years ago I went through something like a spiritual breakdown. I cried, I couldn't sleep, I questioned everything I had done. I'd always believed in God, always embraced the Christian message, but now it seemed that I'd got it all wrong. I was no fool, I knew biblical languages, I read voraciously, I had life experience, but it was as if I'd walked though my life with some sort of comforting theological myopia.

To make matters yet more painful and confusing, in 2013, Uganda's biting homophobia smashed into me. I met some of its victims, wrote about the shame of Christian groups from the United States encouraging and funding some of this, and I spoke out in public on my various media platforms. As a consequence, I was bombarded with abuse and threats. This was nothing, of course, compared to the experience of countless men and women who for so many years have faced such contempt and persecution merely for their sexuality, for being who they are, and as how God made them. And that contempt and persecution continues to this day, especially outside of North America and Western Europe. In some places, God knows how, it's even getting worse. I realized that opposition to equal marriage was based less on defence of traditional marriage than on a visceral dislike, even a manic hatred, of LGBTQ2 people. So, I met with gay Christian groups, who were disarmingly forgiving and loving, I spent as much time as I could with people I had long opposed, I read, I prayed, I wept, I apologized. I changed. That change in this area led, inevitably and exponentially, to change in other areas as well — once the doors of faith are opened, all sorts of things will come tumbling through. Thank the Lord.

In April 2014, I decided to come clean, or at least have a good wash, in my syndicated weekly newspaper column. "In the past six months I have been parachuted into clouds of new realization and empathy regarding gay issues, largely and ironically because of the angry and hateful responses of some people to my defence of persecuted gay men and women in Africa and Russia," I wrote. "This wasn't reasonable opposition but a tainted monomania with no understanding of humanity and an obsession with sex rather than love.... I have evolved on this single subject because I can no longer hide behind comfortable banalities, have realized that love triumphs judgment," and I had realized that a new conversation has to take place, and that the word of God couldn't be, mustn't be, distorted in a way that hurt so, so many people and also their friends and families.

That provoked an outpouring of hostility. There were thousands of emails; letters (some containing bodily waste); death threats; attacks on my family; calls for my wife to leave me; accusations that I was a child abuser, a thief, and a fraud, and that I was doing it all for the money. The latter was particularly odd, in that my professional career largely evaporated in the space of two or three weeks: five regular newspaper columns, fourteen speeches, a book contract, two radio shows, and a television hosting position, all cancelled. There is none so angry as a homophobe scorned. I should have been more intimidated, because this was income, persona, and community all lost within days. But the contrary was true. I felt a sense of empowerment and invigoration. There were volumes of support as well, some of which I will never forget. But doubters too, and fair enough. Apologies aren't sufficient. If we're sorry, we need to show that we're sincere, offer contrition, do penance, and try to compensate for harm done and to repair damage caused. We have to take complete ownership of the sin, and work day and night to put it right.

The point I'm trying to make is that I have been there, been on the conservative side, am familiar with the language and the arguments used, and know that these positions are not reliably scriptural or convincingly Christian. I don't want to chastise or condemn — although something deeply critical is inescapable — but I do want to show that there is a radically different path. I've been trying to do that, to reveal and to walk that path, for eight years now, and finally comes this book. Which is not, I must emphasize, a call to support or join any political party or organization. I'm not a party-political person, and my commitment is exclusively to Jesus Christ and to his teachings. That those teachings lead — in my opinion — to a belief system based around peace, justice, equality, forgiveness, inclusion, humanity, care for the marginalized, poor, and weak, a rejection of materialism, and a commitment to a fundamentally new and different society is the central theme of this text.

So, this book is a partly personal and partly objective and analytical account of the Christian message, and what it says to us today. I make no apologies for the former, because there are more than enough impersonal accounts of Christianity on the market, and also because faith and religion are indeed acutely personal and, in some ways, subjective by their very nature. It must also be emphasized that this book isn't an economic treatise or a sociological study, primarily because the Gospels are built not on economics, sociology, or politics but on romance, on a love affair, and a relationship. Our romance, our love affair, our relationship with Jesus. We love Christ and in turn, as Christians, the first and most central command is to love others. And if that love is to be more than mere emotion and feelings it must involve a profound care for the economic well-being, the physical and mental health, the physical safety, and the dignity and freedom of our fellow creatures. That doesn't mean that we suddenly abandon spiritual concerns — far from it — but it does mean that to separate the care for the soul from the care for the person is not a full Christian response to the Gospels.

The Rebel Christ is an attempt to reposition Christianity not in some radical or strange way but simply and merely in its natural and original form. A reset, a restoration of the Gospel message that has been so twisted, misinterpreted, and even libelled for too long, often by those who claim to follow it most literally. I'm far from the first person to say this, certainly not the greatest, and a long way off from the most noble, but seldom has the time been as ripe and ready as the beginning of the twenty-first century. I say that not with any sort of joy but with great pain and concern. The so-called Christian right has evolved and developed in recent years, becoming an ever-greater force and influence in international politics; we see that all of the time in the United States, of course, but it's also a major factor in other parts of the world. I believe, and I say this with regret rather than anger, that conservative Christians have mangled the authentic meaning of the Christian faith, and also obscured the image of Christianity for non-Christians, who see the religion as ultra-right-wing, and obsessed, as I mentioned earlier, with a handful of hot-button issues such as abortion, LGBTQ2 rights, and assisted dying.

It needn't and shouldn't be that way. For example, what became known as "The Five Marks of Mission" were developed by the Anglican Consultative Council, part of the international Anglican Communion, some years ago. They were adopted by the General Synod of the Church of England in 1996, and many churches now use them, sometimes, though not always, with their own minor edits. They're illustrative because countless Christians of various denominations throughout the world outside of conservative Christianity would embrace them. The five marks of mission are: (1) to proclaim the Good News of the Kingdom; (2) to teach, baptize, and nurture new believers; (3) to respond to human need by loving service; (4) to seek to transform unjust structures of society, to challenge violence of every kind, and to pursue peace and reconciliation; and (5) to strive to safeguard the integrity of creation, and sustain and renew the life of the earth. It's an extremely useful statement, and also a helpful template if we're to understand the more progressive, or realistic, understanding of Jesus. The first two points, the good news of the kingdom — that is, the Gospel story and the Messianic status of Jesus — and the hope to baptize new believers, form the obvious and exclusively Christian element. The following trio concern social and environmental justice, the struggle for peace and liberation, and aspirations that would clearly be considered part of the political left in secular circles. I'd argue that these, however, are as Christ-formed as the first two, but I also know that many Christians would disagree, or would completely change the wording. That, perhaps, is the debate that this book is about.

I don't intend in this brief volume to provide solid or specific economic responses to pressing issues, because much of that depends on direct situations and countries, and is beyond the scope of a book solely about Jesus Christ. Instead, I'll make broader comments based on Christian dynamics. To accept that something is wrong and to resolve to try to put those matters right is the first and most significant step. The question that then has to be asked is whether the various economic and social systems that currently exist reflect the morality and ethics that are implicit in the Gospels.

Nor is this book only about the Gospels and the life of Jesus himself. While the New Testament, and specifically the life of Jesus, will form the centrepiece of my arguments, sometimes I'll refer to the Hebrew Scriptures, the Old Testament, as well. Partly because these often shape the arguments of those who are twisting the Christian message, but also because they informed Jesus, his teachings, and his followers. This isn't a biography of Christ, not a life of Jesus, not an attempt to prove his divinity and to argue the case for Christ as such, but a manifesto or a guide to how his contemporary followers should react to today's major issues in a manner that is soaked in Jesus Christ. Soaked in the being, the life, the teachings, and words of the rebel Christ.

What I write here is certainly not supposed to be a final word about the subject, nor is it written specifically for those deeply inside the circle of theology and its sister subjects. There are many other people writing such books and I wish them well. My intention, I suppose, is to reach a larger and more diverse audience. The point of Gospel truth is that it's supposed to be spread to the entire world, and time is running out, the reputation of organized Christianity is in tatters, and we have to act now if we are to reverse the decline, and to present the Jesus message for everybody, everywhere. I have also only dealt with certain issues, and while I may touch on others in passing, in brief, or indirectly, I do not dwell on them. I spend little time on race, for example, because as a white man I don't think I have the right, the experience, or the qualifications to say too much on that subject; I do not discuss climate change at length, because while it is a pressing Christian issue there are experts elsewhere doing a fine job. What you will see is a mingling of more general conclusions about the Christian case with some in-depth discussions of some of the more political and pertinent issues such as LGBTQ2 equality, women's reproductive rights, and economic justice. All of these, however, discussed from an overwhelmingly Christian perspective. This book is about pure Jesus rather than pure politics.

I should also emphasize that this book isn't about trying to convert people to the Christian faith, but rather to explain what that faith genuinely has to say about vital issues to anybody who has an interest, whatever their religion or lack of one. Of course, if anybody becomes a Christian or develops an interest in Christianity because of the book I'll be delighted. I might not be trying to convert, but I'm certainly not trying to deter! I'm not at all embarrassed to be a follower of Yeshua, and am more than happy to talk about him to anybody who has the time or the inclination.

In addition, while I'm a Christian, and an orthodox one who believes in the teachings of the church, I make here no attempt to prove the claims of Jesus and of his followers about his divinity, or about issues of salvation, belief, and theology. There are more than enough books out there that try to do that, and with far more skill than I could ever display. I do hope, however, that by showing what the real Jesus taught and promoted I can perform a very small part in cleansing the faith from the filth of persecution, abuse, and oppression that has so often accompanied the church and, to a lesser but still agonizing degree, sometimes still does. It is not Jesus who is to blame for these horrors, but those who have twisted and exploited his life and work — that, implicitly, is something that I hope to demonstrate. But sometimes, God forgive us, the harm is too great to be expunged. I fully understand that: but I still stand, I live, and I die with the rebel Christ. I can do no other.

Let me end this introduction with a personal story, and such stories will pepper the book. The corner of two of my city's main streets, on one of those hot summer evenings when everything seems right. To my left is a restaurant, and outside of it a large pile of garbage bags awaiting the morning's pickup. Because of the heat, and because there is decaying food in the bags, the smell is awful. I move away. As I do, though, I see movement. A rat? Surely not so large. Then one of the bags tips forward and I realize that it is a man. A street person has found a safe place to sleep by hiding against a wall, surrounded by bags of stinking garbage.

He hides, of course, because street people are regularly beaten up just for fun. Sometimes they are killed. The thugs believe that nobody really cares, and assume that everyone knows that the cops don't treat such an assault or death the same way they would an attack on a "normal person." That may be an unfair conclusion, or it may not. The man climbs out of the heap, shakes his head, and begins to walk in my direction. He is tiny, a shaking mess and mass of skin and bones. There are open, weeping sores on his face, his clothes are so ripped that I can almost see his genitalia, and he stinks of bodily waste. He comes up to me and in a quiet, frightened voice asks me a question. As he does so his whole body shakes and he is too scared to make eye contact.

"Could you, could you, could you spare some money?" I turn around to answer him and this very gesture of contact makes him shrink back. I respond by asking him a particularly stupid question. I ask if he is hungry. The chances are he isn't going to tell me that he had just dined, and dined at one of the best places in town, and couldn't eat another thing. He says yes, he is hungry. I tell him I'll buy him some food. At which point I begin to walk to the corner store a few yards away so that I, well paid and well fed and one of the world's privileged, can spend a tiny fraction of what I possess to fill this guy's belly for a few hours.

As I walk I see that he is following me. Of course he is. As I would him in such a situation. He wants food, he is regularly lied to and insulted, and I've made a promise. He walks a yard behind me, like some ancient servant in an archaic culture. And as he walks, he trembles and chatters. Stinks. The sickening odour of urine, muck, and decay. The cologne I am wearing probably cost more money that he will see in a lifetime. I'm uncomfortable, embarrassed. Don't know what to say, what to do. People are looking around when they smell him, and they're looking at me. That makes me feel even more uncomfortable, even more embarrassed. We walk into the store. Me with good clothes and a good job. Him with ripped pants and nothing. I take some milk, chips, peanuts, any food that looks vaguely comforting and nourishing. I walk to the counter. He follows. I put the goods down and wait to pay.

The woman working in the store looks pained. There is a can of fresh-air spray underneath the counter, used after street people come into the store so as to expunge the smell. I don't blame her. I might well do the same if I worked there. She pauses, then looks at me. Then at him. Then at me. Then again at him. Then at me again. She seems bewildered, even nervous. A hesitation, and then: "Are you two … are you … are you together. Are you together?" She was asking, of course, if I was paying for this man who looked as though he had not seen money in a very long time. Were we together? Was I together with this man? Were we together? A very sensible and easy question, yet it seemed to take an eternity for the question to register. Only a second, of course. But it was as if the whole world and all of its possibilities suddenly flushed and flashed through my mind. I steadied myself. "Yes," I said. "We are together."

This is the crucial, central question we need to ask ourselves if we are Christians and if we follow Jesus, the rebel Christ. This is the question that Jesus, the rebel Christ, answered all of his life. Is he with us, who are metaphorically broken, stinking, and destitute? He said that he was. Thus we, if we truly know him, have to be together with those who are rejected and detested, with the poor, the hungry, the jobless, the homeless, the abused, the exploited, the suffering. That is what it means to be a Christian. That is what it means to be part of the church, the community, of the rebel Christ.

Chapter 1

Church, Community, the Divide, and the Debate

Who was Jesus, and why do we seem to get him and his teachings so horribly wrong? He was the rebel Christ, who offered something radical, which can be seen today as a joint enterprise of progressive and enlightened people based on the moral agenda we share as believers and non-believers. It's a dedication to the social values that liberate the very people to whom Jesus devoted his work and teachings. He came for everybody but certainly seemed to prefer the poor and needy. He came to provoke the complacent and empower the vulnerable. He was never a figure of the status quo. In fact, Jesus was a revolutionary in his teachings and his actions, introducing us to the world's coruscating possibilities, and catapulting us into new areas of imagination and understanding. His parents were a young, poor Jewish couple living under imperial occupation who were forced to find a makeshift shelter for their baby to be born. It may or may not have been a stable, perhaps a spare room with animals close by, or a cave, of which there are many in the Bethlehem I know well. It was probably not snowy, there are discrepancies about dates and agricultural conditions, but if you think that this matters you're rather missing the point. It's not when or how but *that* it occurred.

As Christians we believe that this was a planned and divine act, that magic entered the world through the Son of God, the creator taking on the most vulnerable and needy form of a baby, to show heavenly solidarity with a suffering humanity. That baby grows into manhood, and sings a grand, sweeping poem of love, peace, justice, grace, forgiveness, hope, equality, revolution, understanding, and change. Sings, not shouts. A gentle rabbi whose life and beliefs seem so dramatically different from the harshness and intolerance of politicized Christians. And born in an age when cruelty and confusion abounded, but born, I believe, the Son of God, to bathe the world in shades of grace and hope. Who, as a man, would insist that it was love rather than power, humility rather than pride, and peace rather than war that could change and save the world. Christmas trees have non-Christian origins, and even the festival itself may have been designed to be celebrated at the winter solstice to appeal to the recently converted in ancient Europe. That's all old news, and all irrelevant to the central meaning. Whenever I'm in Bethlehem with my Palestinian Christian friends they joke about North American atheists casting doubt and thus threatening their tourist trade. "Come on, man, haven't we suffered enough at the hands of you guys?" They joke a lot, because otherwise they would weep.

So, the coming of Jesus into the world is, with apologies to conspiracy theorists everywhere, the great reset. It's a divine reminder to a complacent and selfish humanity that we have a purpose and a meaning, that everybody is precious, and that if we are indeed made in the image of God we all have a right to be treated with dignity and respect. The poor and the weak, victims of racism, the different, those who have — with bitter irony — suffered at the hands of ostensible Christians who have colonized their land. The rebel Christ should prompt us to question our behaviour, to become participants in the great gospel revolution of empathy and goodness. Because he was the revolutionary majestic. Not a traditionalist, but someone who questioned authority and scolded those who judged others and stood behind smugness and legalism. The Jesus portrayed too often today is a caricature who has more in common with Nordic pagan gods than the Jewish Messiah. He is frequently abused and exploited to justify hatred and fear, and that is the greatest sin of all.

We are required by him, demanded by him, to stand with the marginalized, rethink and improve ourselves, and engage the world as disciples of equality and community. We are warned time and time again to be wary of the sanctuary of religious conservatism, and to welcome the shock of the new, that is inherent in the Christian faith. It's difficult. Bloody difficult. As G.K. Chesterton once wrote, "The Christian ideal has not been tried and found wanting. It has been found difficult; and left untried." It's not easy, it wasn't supposed to be, and if anybody finds it so they're not doing it right. I realize that to those who reject Christianity this may all seem nonsense, and I thank God you are able to believe and proclaim that; I only ask that you have the same respect and patience for those of us who disagree, and regard this book in the same manner. I'm as frustrated and disappointed by triumphalist religiosity as any doubter or atheist — perhaps more so, because it so shames the faith I hold so strongly and so deeply.

Jesus came to care about everybody, and when he did become angry it was at those who judge and condemn, who obsess about scriptural pedantry, who place law above love, and who refuse to embrace the gospel command that we live in community, and with the values of peace, equality, inclusion, justice, and hope. Yes, you'll hear those words used repeatedly in the book, and I make no apologies for it. We can never, ever hear them enough, especially when so many Christians appear to have forgotten what they mean. That transforming position, that transforming belief system, also means that we must turn the other cheek, carry the bags of an enemy, put others first, reject materialism, and forgive not once but forever. That is what Jesus teaches, and it is where strength comes in. It is extraordinarily difficult to do any of that properly, and so much easier to follow the crowd, or to scream about abortion, or assisted dying, the alleged decline of family values, and gay marriage. But the authentic Christian should break rather than observe the established rules, and is called not to preserve the status quo but to turn it upside down. That is the tune of the Gospels, those are the lyrics of the cross, and that is the melody of the resurrection. God does not guarantee a good or an easy life, but does promise a perfect eternity.

Yet this picture is so dramatically different from the Christianity we see proclaimed so readily. Let's set the picture. The administration of Donald Trump ended just a short while ago. The president of the United States, the most powerful man in the world, was replaced by his opponent, Joe Biden. But before this, as the 2020 election approached, the enormously influential Christian evangelist Franklin Graham, son of the iconic Billy and president of the Billy Graham Evangelistic Association and the charity Samaritan's Purse, wrote to his 2.3 million followers of the threat of "all-out socialism" if Americans didn't vote for leaders who "love this country, defend the Constitution, and support law & order." In other words, their Christian duty was to vote for Donald Trump and his followers. Graham had once again, along with so many of his colleagues within the church, held up the teachings of Jesus as contrary to socialism, liberalism, and all that is progressive, and even described them as a bulwark against these ideas. In all honesty, none of that came as very much of a surprise, in that Graham has in the past argued that Muslims should be banned from the United States because Islam is "very evil and wicked," and that LGBTQ2 people should be barred from churches because Satan "wants to devour our homes." He had also stated after the presidential election in 2016 that the triumph of Donald Trump was due to the "hand of God," and had lauded Vladimir Putin for "protecting Russian young people against homosexual propaganda." Pretty awful stuff, but we can't just dismiss it, because Franklin Graham speaks for an enormous number of Christians, and they regard him as a crucial advocate for Jesus Christ.

Graham is not alone, of course. Most on the Christian right in North America, and abroad, championed Donald Trump and even continue to do so, and see the hand of evil in anybody who opposes the Republican leader. In January 2021, a hysterical mob charged the Capitol Building in Washington, DC, intent on overthrowing the democratically elected government, leading to five deaths at the time and two suicides later as a result of what happened, and to tens of thousands of troops having to enter the area so as to guarantee law and order. Among the rioters were many people wearing shirts emblazoned "Jesus Saves," and waving large flags with the same message. While not all in the mob were Christian, a great many were, and claimed that their Christian faith was the motivating factor for their criminal and treasonous behaviour. They even held an impromptu prayer service in the Senate chamber!

Yet Donald Trump is an adulterer, a liar, and a bully. He was a supremely divisive and dangerous president, and an appalling role model for those around him. This didn't seem to matter, however, for the more than 80 percent of white born-again or evangelical Christians and millions of Roman Catholics who voted for him, and the vast, overwhelming majority of white evangelical Protestants who still back him. He is held up by numerous Christian leaders as a protector of the faith, and a great man of God. So, it's no surprise that many progressive people, and those outside of the church, believe that organized Christianity stands in direct opposition to the aspirations of liberal change, social democracy, and the creation of a more fair, gentle, kind, and tolerant society. It would be bad enough if the problem were just Donald Trump, but the malaise goes far deeper than that. Across the United States, Christian leaders endorse conservative politicians, often of the harshest kind, and condemn their opponents as being untrustworthy, and even immoral or, quite literally, the agents of Satan. The devil was unavailable for comment during the writing of this book. Outside of the U.S. the situation is not always dissimilar. Conservative Christians have rallied about ultra-right-wing Brazilian leader Jair Bolsonaro. In Canada, Christian activist Charles McVety endorsed the conservative premier of Ontario, Doug Ford, and megachurch leader Paul Melnichuk anointed the same right-wing populist as "a man surely the Lord has visited." McVety, by the way, had a show on a Christian TV network cancelled in 2010 for suggesting that LGBTQ2 people prey on children, and Melnichuk was denounced by the Canadian Jewish Congress over a sermon in which he labelled Jews "the most miserable people in the whole world." He later apologized, so that's okay …

Evangelical Christians and conservative Catholics are also standing for political office in ever-greater numbers, convinced that they can no longer stand back from a political process that is destroying Christendom. Alastair Campbell, adviser to former British prime minister Tony Blair, once famously said, "We don't do God." Politicians in much of the rest of the world "don't do God" either, but Americans of both major parties do so in abundance. One of the ironies of the United States is that a country that so boasts about the concept of the separation of church and state has a political system so coated in religiosity. Christians vote in enormous numbers and many U.S. politicians are genuine believers, whatever their party allegiance.

The case of Donald Trump, however, is especially poignant because it's still alive, kicking, and biting, and because his tens of millions of followers are still convinced that God is very much on their side. Yet it's hardly a secret that his personal behaviour and political positions were and remain so jarring for someone who says he's a Christian. They appear, in fact, to be the direct antithesis of the Gospel values of peace, love, humility, and justice.

Who can forget, for example, in the early summer of 2020 when Trump had massed ranks of police violently disperse non-violent protesters so that he could walk from his news conference in the rose garden of the White House to St. John's Episcopal Church. He stood in front of this historic church, renowned for its commitment to social justice, held a Bible, and posed ostentatiously for the cameras. Just yards away, young people who had been demonstrating against racist violence and the murder of George Floyd wept with tears produced by tear gas and by frustration. Yet Donald Trump, supremely indifferent and even mocking, held high the text of love, peace, and justice. This was blasphemy. In the most authentic and repugnant sense, it was blasphemy.

The Rt. Rev. Mariann Budde, bishop of the Episcopal Diocese of Washington that includes St. John's, put it well when she said that neither she nor the priest at the church had been consulted, and that she was

> outraged that they would be clearing with tear gas so they could use one of our churches as a prop. Holding a bible, one that declares that God is love and when everything he has said and done is to enflame violence. We need moral leadership and he's done everything to divide us and has just used one of the most sacred symbols of the Judeo-Christian tradition. We so disassociate ourselves from the messages of this president. We hold the teachings of our sacred texts to be so grounding to our lives and everything we do and it is about love of neighbour and sacrificial love and justice.

But surely even with Donald Trump supporting conservative Christians on most of these subjects, they must have realized that his ostensible commitment to their cause was conveniently recent, and his private life and treatment of other people is far from what is required of a believing Christian? Many, though not all, did. But the answer as to why they could ignore the contradiction, or even the hypocrisy, reveals part of the problem of the contemporary conservative Christian mind. They've tried to give a historical or theological veneer to their support, arguing that Trump was the modern equivalent of Emperor Constantine or King Cyrus II. The former was a Roman Caesar in the early fourth century, a late convert to Christianity who gave the church fervent support. The latter was a Persian monarch twenty-five hundred years ago, who allowed the conquered Jewish people to return to Jerusalem and rebuild the temple. Both men were deeply flawed, but traditionalists would claim they empowered God's plan — and thus the comparison. While President Trump may have behaved appallingly, he enabled goodness to flourish by fighting abortion, supporting Israel, defending what evangelicals regard as their personal freedoms, including gun rights, and defending Christians who claimed that they were being persecuted.

Israel's *Haaretz* newspaper put it thus: "Trump was already a hero to a wide swath of evangelicals … But the role he's playing in what many believe is the fulfillment of divine prophecy has gotten him promoted to king for some of them — an ancient Persian king to be precise. For his willingness to confront conventional diplomatic wisdom, shrug off dire warnings of triggering Middle East unrest and declare Jerusalem Israel's capital, Trump is increasingly being compared by evangelicals … to Persia's King Cyrus … the Great."

Intellectual Takeout is a leading media platform for conservative and libertarian views. It argued that: "America doesn't need a president to make arguments for us. America just needs a president to give us the freedom to make our arguments without fear of being shouted down by the politically correct brigade. Whatever else you might say about Trump, he is definitely politically incorrect, and prides himself on that attribute. He refuses to back down after making controversial statements. He does not apologize for offending groups after making arguments. He stands up to the media. He is defiant in spite of being vilified by political elites, journalists, and academics."

Right-wing Christians have engineered an almost parallel version of the faith, one that is based around a collection of specific themes. First, religious freedom, viewed from a perspective that balks even at limitations on the size of church gatherings to protect public health during the Covid-19 pandemic. Second, gun rights, with armed self-reliance seen as a biblical virtue, when in fact Jesus is regarded as the Prince of Peace. Third, support for Israel, not because they're especially pro-Jewish but due to an eschatology that looks to an end-times war between Israel and its enemies leading to the Second Coming. Fourth, resistance to LGBTQ2 equality, in terms of marriage, civil rights, and even social acceptance. Fifth, a deep, visceral, obsessive, and sometimes even violent objection to abortion. Anybody who can appeal to these triggers is certain to motivate the conservative Christian base.

Then there is the simple dishonesty. For example, in 2020 Fox News host Laura Ingraham messaged her 3.5 million Twitter followers: "Will Joe Biden do more to protect religious liberty than Donald Trump? Not a prayer. 'City of Toronto Bans Catholic Churches From Administering Holy Communion'" and then linked to an article by an obscure right-wing writer named Shane Trejo. He'd written, "The city of Toronto has announced that they will be banning the sacrament of holy communion in Catholic Churches, using the Covid-19 pandemic as an excuse to attack religious liberty." He went on to discuss "Canada's war on Christianity, which has seen pastors arrested for preaching the Gospel in public after being attacked by soulless LGBT degenerates." That ugly sentence was actually about the eventual arrest, after several warnings, of a high-profile anti-LGBTQ2 activist for the crime of disturbing the peace.

A rude and extreme unknown is one thing but Ingraham is another. As irresponsible and hyperbolic as she may be, the author and broadcaster has enormous influence, especially in the Christian world. Her comments about Joe Biden come as no surprise but the truth is that he's certainly far more rooted in his faith than Donald Trump, is a regular communicant, and once considered a vocation to the Catholic priesthood. On the issue of the ban Ingraham claimed to be happening in Canada, however, this is nothing more than total fabrication; something I know well because I am a cleric who lives in the city.

Cardinal Collins, Roman Catholic archbishop of Toronto, had merely written in a letter to his flock that "in view of the requirements of the Government of Ontario, during this medical emergency, I instruct that all public Masses be cancelled, both during the week and on the weekend. Churches will be available for individual private prayer." He continued, "Perhaps this sacrifice will help us to cherish more profoundly the great gift of the Holy Eucharist" and, "While it is a painful moment in the life of the Church to take these extreme measures, we pray that they will aid in combating the pandemic that has affected so many in our own community and around the world."

There had been prolonged consultation before the government acted, and mainstream churches and other religious bodies were in full agreement with the policy. It was, they agreed, an issue of caring for one's neighbour. So, the conservative Christian response was simply propaganda, and yet another example of the irresponsible, dangerous, and dishonest abuse of Christianity; an attempt to claim some sort of moral authority, and to depict opponents of the Christian right as the enemies of God.

So, it's all a bit of a mess, to say the least. And it's not at all surprising that those who are liberal or left wing, or simply moderate and reasonable, have given up on Christianity because of how it's so often presented. They see it as a distraction from the genuine challenges of the world, and of the problems of poverty, unemployment, the despair of so many young people, and sheer need. Karl Marx didn't actually say, as is often claimed, that said faith was the "opiate of the people." He said, "Religion is the sigh of the oppressed creature, the heart of a heartless world, and the soul of soulless conditions. It is the opium of the people." In other words, religion has been used as an alternative to social justice, a justification for lack of equality and economic decency. Faith has been abused. As such, he has a lot in common with the rebel Christ. (Groucho Marx didn't comment, although I so wish he had.)

We're seldom surprised when we see yet another example of how Christians can get it all so tragically wrong, and that dichotomy between how Christians should behave and how some of them actually do was brought into sharp focus in the midst of the Covid-19 crisis. It's worth mentioning because it's so current. In general, the vast majority of churches, internationally, closed their doors completely or partly, acted responsibly, put their services online, and reached out to congregants to offer help and support. It was impressive, swift, and responsible. Most churches — but not all.

On the conservative fringes of Christianity — Catholic, Protestant, and Orthodox — church leaders resisted and rejected the lockdown for various reasons. Some saw it all as state intervention, and embraced an eschatological horror of the government telling them what to do. In some cases, such as the Orthodox Church in Russia, it was partly understandable in that under Communism the state was a persecuting oppressor. In others, especially in North America, it was largely the stuff of right-wing rhetoric and fundamentalist theology: government is evil by nature if not positively satanic, the virus is a hoax, God will not allow harm to come to people who worship in church, the alcohol in the sacramental wine kills the disease, and as one woman in Ohio told CNN as she was leaving church, she wasn't worried because "I'm covered in Jesus' blood." In California, a group of pastors filed a lawsuit against Governor Gavin Newsom and local officials, claiming that the "stay-at-home" policy was contrary to the U.S. Constitution because it criminalized "the free exercise of religion." Other church leaders across North America have been fined and even arrested for holding church meetings.

Florida megachurch pastor Rodney Howard-Browne, for example, was arrested for holding two services involving hundreds of people. Louisiana pastor Tony Spell was arrested for holding services where twenty-six buses brought worshippers to his church. The list goes on. More than a dozen U.S. states made places of worship exceptions in their lockdowns, partly due to political pressure from the evangelical lobby. One doesn't want to appear cynical, but it's worth remembering that these large churches take in enormous amounts of donation money each Sunday. In Paris, France, the ultra-conservative Society of St. Pius X, a breakaway Roman Catholic group with some extremely right-wing beliefs, staged a Latin-rite Easter service, and images from the ceremony showed numerous people clustered together, all ignoring safety precautions. The priest was fined.

In Canada, there was a general acceptance of the realities of the virus and need for a lockdown among more conservative churches, although some in the somewhat strident Catholic anti-abortion community — not particularly supportive of Pope Francis or anything that appears in any way progressive — expressed outrage at Mass being suspended for the laity. A petition signed by a number of leading Catholics was circulated, stating, "Something is terribly wrong with a culture that allows abortion clinics and liquor stores to remain open but shuts down places of worship." One high-profile case saw six members of Trinity Bible Chapel in Waterloo, Ontario, charged for breaching the province's lockdown restrictions. "For years, we have taught our children to respect police, and now our children and grandchildren are witness to their fathers and grandfathers receiving charges from police for worshipping Christ with our church," responded the church in a press release. "It is a dark day for Waterloo Region and Ontario." It added that the lockdown was "an unconstitutional and unlawful restriction of religious freedom."

It was all political hyperbole, of course, but within it there was a greater, more interesting question to be asked about priorities and about freedom of worship. Then and now we assume certain liberties as a given in modern society, and religious toleration is certainly one of them. This was a world crisis, and rational consensus understands the needs for social isolation; but we do allow people to shop, so why not also allow them to praise and pray? The answer is that we do. Freedom of worship was not restricted, merely the right to assemble in churches and thus increase the likelihood of the spread of infection. Such a spread doesn't only endanger the person who decides to attend church, but also the innocent other party whom the worshipper then meets. This division of understanding of what it means to be a Christian, and to live as a Christian in the greater world, demonstrates just how deep is the chasm between conservative followers of the church, and friends of the rebel Christ.

A great deal of the negative Christian reaction was more hysterical than holy, and while the extremists were relatively few in number and far from sophisticated, they were noisy and well connected. The loudest splashes, we are told, are always in the shallow end of the swimming pool. But, once again, the public face of Christianity was distorted. As if this wasn't bad enough, there were also Christian leaders who saw Covid-19 as some form of divine punishment for the world's apparently sad journey toward utter darkness and destruction, or, as others might see it, its steady progress toward enlightenment and acceptance.

Historically, there have always been Christians who looked for scapegoats (Jews, foreigners, witches, whomever) when plague or disasters occurred, and others who were convinced that it was all a punishment from God for our sins. Those sins tend to vary according to the political climate of the day. Back in 2014 Texas televangelist John Hagee said that the Ebola outbreak was God's punishment for President Barack Obama's policies about Israel; and, after 9/11, Jerry Falwell and Pat Robertson claimed on U.S. television that God had allowed the terror attack because the Lord Almighty was angry with America for encouraging abortion, homosexuality, and secular education.

Then there was AIDS. Because in the western world the virus was particularly hideous and common among gay men and intravenous drug users, the Christian right saw God's hand at work. God forgive them! My personal theory is that God's punishment for our sins is that we have to listen to hysterical fanatics screaming that God is punishing us for our sins.

One would have hoped that all of this would change over the years, but not so. Robert Jeffress is the pastor of Dallas First Baptist Church, which boasts fourteen thousand worshippers. He is also a regular Fox News contributor and was one of Donald Trump's favourite ministers. He preached a sermon entitled, "Is the Coronavirus a Judgment From God?" In it, at first it looked like we were going to be okay: "The coronavirus is not one of the plagues in Revelation," he explained. But hold on just one fundamentalist moment. Jeffress continued, "All natural disasters can ultimately be traced to sin." Damn! (as it were).

LifeSite, one of the most influential conservative Christian media platforms in the world, of course had its say. It ran a column with the headline, "Coronavirus is 'the killer of globalization' and a 'scourge' from God: Roberto de Mattei," and then described Catholic historian de Mattei as a "celebrated intellectual." The article went on to quote the man without any attempt at criticism or disagreement. "God is righteous and rewarding and gives to each what is his due: he not only chastises individual persons but he also sends tribulations to families, cities, and nations for the sins which they commit." *LifeSite* also listed as one of its featured blogs an article headlined, "Why coronavirus is a punishment from God that should lead to repentance." The author wrote, "It is true that those who suffer most are not necessarily the greatest sinners, but the explanation of this is the familiar idea that the punishment God sends us is a sign of love." Personally, I prefer a nice card, a box of chocolates, and some roses.

At a more serious or theological level, this is a reductive and banal spirituality that may satisfy the zealot but is dangerously crass and in fact profoundly ungodly. It depicts a genocidal God, sufficiently cruel to hurt indiscriminately, and too indifferent or impotent to be able to punish only those who have genuinely caused harm. It's all the product of an ancient, fearful belief system that has nothing to do with Jesus, and is so distant and different from the Gospel calls to turn the other cheek, embrace our enemies, reach out to the most rejected and marginalized, and work for justice and peace.

Let's talk a little about that Bible, or more to the point, about the Bible in general. The word actually means "library," a collection of books written over centuries by many different people, and containing works of history, metaphor, poetry, and literal truth. I believe it to be inspired by God but not to be divine dictation; I read it as a wonderful guide to many of the great moral issues but it's not a handbook for every aspect of daily living. It must be combined with experience, understanding, and faith. But most of all it is holy, and at the centre of every Christian's life. It's not a tool, not a product to be marketed like some worthless trinket on a television game show.

There are various translations of the Bible, and the one I've used in this book is the New Revised Standard Version (NRSV). It's more gender-inclusive than some others, it's scholarly, and it conveys the passion of the text. Translation matters, whatever the book, and with the Bible this is even more complex because this is a sacred work containing stories and accounts that shape lives, cultures, nations, and souls. We're speaking here of nuanced and multi-faceted books and stories, containing history, poetry, metaphor and truth, miracle and anecdote, guides on how to live, and accounts of how others failed to live. It's also the case that we know more now about who wrote Scripture, why they wrote it, and what they meant by it than at any time since it was first read. Generations of biblical archaeology, linguistic discoveries, and historical research have made us far more knowledgeable about these ancient texts than in the past, and if we filter all of this through the modern prisms of contemporary science, sociology, and human understanding we are, in effect, the most-equipped biblical scholars in history.

It shouldn't be, can't be, denied that countless conservative Christians do reach out to the poor and the homeless on an individual if not structural basis. What they lack, I would argue, is an understanding, or acceptance, of the need for more systemic change. Yes, they might have a deep faith that permeates all they are and all that they try to do, and in that regard sometimes put other Christians to shame. Yet, underlying that absolute commitment to religion is a clinical, harsh code of right and wrong. They would do well, instead, to heed the words of Dietrich Bonhoeffer, the Lutheran martyr to Nazism: "We are not to simply bandage the wounds of victims beneath the wheels of injustice, we are to drive a spoke into the wheel itself."

Some of these Christians are Protestant and embrace the literal truth of the Bible; others are Roman Catholic and look to the teachings of the magisterium (the all-powerful teaching office of the Catholic Church). Yet, because of their common anxiety and fear about a world they see as becoming increasingly immoral, we now have a strange unity, a strange ecumenism, where conservative Protestants and conservative Catholics have more in common with one another than they do with the liberal members of their respective churches. This is nothing less than a startling development, one that Canadian poet and novelist Maggie Helwig, who has served as an Anglican priest in downtown Toronto since 2012, describes as "a different kind of protest movement" — one "based in a kind of panic fear about a situation in which Christianity is no longer hegemonic." The result, she says, is a theology that "mobilizes the worst authoritarian and punitive tendencies in Christian theology" in the face of what its adherents have come to define as "terrific existential danger if certain rigid boundaries are transgressed."

Then there is the intellectual vacuum. "The scandal of the evangelical mind," in the words of Mark Noll, one of the most respected historians of the evangelical world, "is that there is not much of an evangelical mind." It wasn't always that way. The early Protestant movement prided itself on being the thinking branch of Christendom. The Puritans established universities in colonial America, and seventeenth-century British dictator Oliver Cromwell — who cut off the king's head and banned Christmas (too wasteful, too papal) — employed the faithful and, of course, brilliant John Milton as one of his secretaries.

While, in Catholic circles, a belief in intellectual excellence still exists (although it tends to be far stronger among Jesuits and Dominicans), evangelical culture has retreated from the world — and, perhaps more disturbingly, is working to erect a parallel one that is run according to its own laws and logic. Which is why we see a new wave of Christian high schools and colleges. But too often these institutions are dominated by single issues. Indeed, for many Catholics, too, the loathing of abortion, no matter the circumstances, trumps even the most basic of Christian virtues. In 2015, in the *Prairie Messenger*, a Catholic newspaper in Western Canada, I wrote a column about a ten-year-old Paraguayan girl who had been denied an abortion after being raped by her stepfather. I supported the poor child, and said that she should indeed have the abortion. I was promptly fired (albeit amid profuse apologies from my editor, who cited external pressure). Which in turn prompted a major Christian media platform to announce that they were "glad that *Prairie Messenger* will no longer be a mouthpiece for Coren's misplaced notions of compassion and love." Imagine: compassion and love for a pregnant ten-year-old having no place at the Christian table.

Bishop Kallistos Ware, an English convert to Eastern Orthodoxy, who for many years was a lecturer at Oxford University, wrote that, "It is not the task of Christianity to provide easy answers to every question, but to make us progressively aware of a mystery," and "God is not so much the object of our knowledge as the cause of our wonder." That wonder is troubling for those who want easy answers as to why the world is not like it was, who want their faith neatly packaged in catechismal certainty. But being born again is not the same as being born yesterday, and questioning is not the same as denying. As scientific knowledge expands and public attitudes change, Christianity today must either respond intelligently and constructively, or retreat into an ever-shrinking, more hostile hobbit-hole of irrelevance.

The coming years will see a new generation of believers assuming positions of influence and authority in our churches and in our society. Those leaders will have the option of building walls or building bridges, of extending the circle so as to include as many people as possible or standing at the corners of their creeds and repelling all they see as a threat. Of lending a hand to the marginalized and needy, or withdrawing it once and for all. James E. Wallis Jr. is a Christian writer and political activist, best known as the founder and editor of *Sojourners* magazine, a journal of the evangelical left. He writes: "Two of the greatest hungers in our world today are the hunger for spirituality and the hunger for social change. The connection between the two is the one the world is waiting for, especially the new generation. And the first hunger will empower the second."

Whether Christians will listen to Mr. Wallis — or, for that matter, to Jesus Christ — remains to be seen. Their decision will influence all of us, whatever our faith or lack thereof. And it will determine whether our houses of worship, and our houses of politics, are places of division and discord — or living rooms where love is always welcome and compassion finds a home.

A few words about how we read the Bible before we end this chapter. Scripture needs to be read and understood intelligently and carefully. It is quite clearly wrong, anti-intellectual, crass, and downright dangerous to read any historical, or even current document for that matter, without understanding its context, purpose, setting, author, vocabulary, and style. If we take satire, parody, or caricature, for example, as being literally true we get into all sorts of serious trouble. Words have meaning and meanings have words. Language is also mutable and what particular words and language meant even a generation or two ago can be different from a contemporary understanding. So imagine the challenges and possible difficulty of understanding words written thousands of years ago in various languages.

I'll end this "setting of the scene" with a personal story. When my mum, Sheila Coren, was in the final stages of her dementia I would sit by her bed and silently ask how this could be allowed to happen. This good, kind woman was now a shell of what she was, unable to speak her pain and fear, oblivious to the love and care that was around her. Where was God, why was such horror happening to one so undeserving? Such questions have been asked for all time, and are still being uttered in agonized choruses. I was just the latest in a very long line, indeed. In theology this problem of God and the existence of human suffering is known as "theodicy" and there are entire books written about it. But in all honesty it's just a way to intellectualize what is an entirely justifiable scream of sorrow and anger.

The letter of James in the Bible tells us to be patient and confident in our suffering, and C.S. Lewis wrote of pain being God's "megaphone to rouse a deaf world." Yet while this might be helpful, it can't and doesn't explain the death of a child or the horror of a parent. As for those ghouls who insist that it's all a punishment for our sins, like some of those mentioned earlier in this chapter, that's twisting God into a personal vigilante and is shameful. It's also directly contrary to what Jesus said about the sick. He spent an extraordinary amount of time with the ill and the disabled, and totally rejected any idea that their plight was a result of their or their family's actions. But it still doesn't answer the question of why all this happens, and it's in no way inappropriate to wonder at a God who is supposed to be all powerful, all good, and all knowing.

A mature faith allows for questions as well as for answers, even encourages them, and if anybody wants a complete and satisfying answer I simply cannot give one. I'd also recommend being extremely dubious about any person of faith who claimed otherwise. This isn't some philosophical game. My response, for what it's worth, is that this life is not all that there is, and that this is only the land of shadows. I have hope because I know that Jesus suffered too, and that the resurrection was the template for all of humanity. I realize this might be inadequate for the non-Christian, even for some Christians, but let me also emphasize that I'm convinced that Jesus came not only for his followers but for everybody.

There's more. He was us. Was us, and is us. The Christian belief is that Jesus was fully God but also fully human, and knew our pain and terror not as a divine onlooker but as part of the human community.

This was the unique, the unprecedented miracle of divine empathy. The heavenly leap of God into our lives and our deaths. He wept and he loved, for us and with us. The world in which Jesus lived was soaked in bloody injustice, oppression, and often gruesome death, and surely it's no accident that this was the time chosen for God to break into humanity. That gives me enormous solace, even when all around me is brokenness and chaos.

My mum eventually fell into a coma-like sleep, and the dementia took her while she was alone in a distant hospital ward. I wouldn't insult you by claiming that it was all somehow tolerable because of my faith. Mum wasn't a Christian; Mum suffered, and I was angry and I was crushed. What I will say is that hope is the great conqueror, and that I know that love wins in the end. It is that conviction that helps me believe that the real Christ, the authentic Christ, the genuine Christ, will become increasingly apparent, and that his teachings will give answers to us all. It's why I wrote this book, and why I follow the rebel Christ.

Chapter 2

Jesus Hates Commies

Problem is, he doesn't. And communism, a construct of many centuries later, has nothing to do with it. But Jesus was repeatedly, consistently, and undeniably socialistic, if we allow an anachronism, in his actions and teaching; and much to the frustration of the political right, which embraces an increasingly harsh individualism, Jesus believed in the collective. In fact, at the heart of the Christian rebellion are the absolutes of community and fraternity, mentioned repeatedly in the Gospels, and in the various letters of St. Paul and others contained in the New Testament that were written to the early church. I'd like to begin this chapter with seven quotations about this subject — seven, after all, being considered the most biblical of numbers.

"The bread you do not use is the bread of the hungry. The garment hanging in your wardrobe belongs to him who is naked. The shoes you do not wear are the shoes of those who are barefoot. The money you keep locked away is the money of the poor. The acts of charity you do not perform are so many injustices you commit."

"Give to everyone that asks, without looking for any repayment, for it is the Father's pleasure that we should share His gracious bounty with all men. A giver who gives freely, as the commandment directs, is blessed; no fault can be found with him."

"All things belong to God, the Father of us and them. We are all of the same stock, all brothers. And when men are brothers, the best and most equitable thing is that they should inherit equal portions."

"We, who loved above all else the ways of acquiring riches and possessions, now hand over to a community fund what we possess and share it with every needy person."

"May God preserve me from being rich while they are indigent, from enjoying robust health if I do not try to cure their diseases, from eating good food, clothing myself well and resting in my home if I do not share with them a piece of my bread and give them, in the measure of my abilities, part of my clothes and if I do not welcome them into my home."

"The need to resolve the structural causes of poverty cannot be delayed, not only for the pragmatic reason of its urgency for the good order of society, but because society needs to be cured of a sickness which is weakening and frustrating it, and which can only lead to new crises. Welfare projects, which meet certain urgent needs, should be considered merely temporary responses. As long as the problems of the poor are not radically resolved by rejecting the absolute autonomy of markets and financial speculation and by attacking the structural causes of inequality, no solution will be found for the world's problems or, for that matter, to any problems. Inequality is the root of social ills."

"Even when they call us mad, when they call us subversives and communists and all the epithets they put on us, we know we only preach the subversive witness of the Beatitudes, which have turned everything upside down."

Pretty radical, collectivist, and — even to some — Marxist stuff. Yet the first is from St. Basil the Great, the second is taken from the *Didache*, the third is by Gregory of Nyssa, the fourth is Justin Martyr, the fifth said by Gregory of Nazianzus, the sixth is Pope Francis, and the seventh a statement by Oscar Romero. Pope Francis may not need an introduction, but the others likely do. Basil the Great, or Basil of Caesarea, was a fourth-century bishop and theologian known for his opposition to heresy and his inspired defence of the seminal Nicene Creed, still used today in churches the world over. The *Didache*, or "The Lord's Teaching Through the Twelve Apostles to the Nations," is a first-century Christian treatise written in koine Greek, and one of the earliest and most reliable accounts of the early church that we have.

Gregory of Nyssa was bishop of Nyssa in the late fourth century. He is considered a saint in the Roman Catholic, Eastern Orthodox, Oriental Orthodox, Anglican, and Lutheran churches. Justin Martyr was a second-century Christian apologist and thinker, a saint, and one of the most important philosophers in all of Christian history. Gregory of Nazianzus was archbishop of Constantinople in the fourth century and regarded as one of the finest stylists of the age. Oscar Romero was a courageous and gifted prelate of the Roman Catholic Church in El Salvador, who was murdered in 1980 because of his Christian activism for the oppressed and impoverished. He is a modern martyr of the faith.

But none were Donald Trump's buddy "MyPillow Guy," Jerry Falwell, or even Pat Robertson.

The point is that it's not new, novel, or nonsense to claim that Christianity is based on a dramatically socialistic and radical reinterpretation of ownership, property, profit, money, and power. Forgive the number of quotations in this chapter, but it's important to set the framework and underline the reality of what is being discussed here. Reluctant as I am to "Bible-bash," it's essential if we're to "bash" away at the propaganda around Christianity that has developed, especially in the last few decades.

This is worth noting, because the association of conservatism with Christianity is in fact fairly recent, and in North America part of this link can be traced back to the fight for prohibition before the

Second World War. The conservative evangelical movement enjoyed their greatest success in the 1920s and early '30s with the achievement of banning the sale of alcohol, but such was the resistance to the move, and its relative failure in that it divided the country and also empowered organized crime and the gangster culture, that right-wing Christianity rather withdrew from the political sphere for more than a generation. The movement was politically and spiritually exhausted, embarrassed by its loss of reputation and the eventual failure of its chosen cause, and the political field was left to liberal Christians, both Protestant and Catholic. It was not until the 1960s and the so-called social revolution and permissive society that conservative churches began to reorganize politically as a direct reaction to what they saw as the decadence around them. In Britain, the Labour Party was always said to have owed more to Methodism than to Marxism, and while there were, of course, numerous Christians on the political right, many and sometimes most of the socialist parties around the world had some form of connection to Christianity. William Temple, who was archbishop of Canterbury during the second half of the Second World War, went so far as to say that, "Socialism is the economic realization of the Christian gospel."

Consider for a moment the origins of the Christian story. Joseph and Mary are young people who live under an imperial regime than occupies their homeland, and exploits them economically and politically. Remember, God doesn't make mistakes and the setting of the holy story, and the coming into the world of Jesus at such a time and in such a place, cannot be and isn't just an accident, a chance happening. The Christian belief is that there is always reason and purpose behind Scripture. The young couple is forced to flee, as refugees, to have their child in a faraway place, without resources, and dependent on the goodwill of others. Their child grows to be someone who, according to British writer and critic Terry Eagleton, was "homeless, propertyless, peripatetic, socially marginal, disdainful of kinfolk, without a trade or occupation, a friend of outcasts and pariahs, averse to material possessions, without fear for his own safety, a thorn in the side of the establishment and a scourge of the rich and powerful."

Beyond what others have thought and said about Christ, consider his own words, and here is where we bash that Bible. In Mark 10:21–25, a rich man asks him what he must do to inherit eternal life. The answer is shocking even now.

> Jesus, looking at him, loved him and said, "You lack one thing; go, sell what you own, and give the money to the poor, and you will have treasure in heaven; then come, follow me." When he heard this, he was shocked and went away grieving, for he had many possessions. Then Jesus looked around and said to his disciples, "How hard it will be for those who have wealth to enter the kingdom of God!" And the disciples were perplexed at these words. But Jesus said to them again, "Children, how hard it is to enter the kingdom of God! It is easier for a camel to go through the eye of a needle than for someone who is rich to enter the kingdom of God."

In Matthew 19, there is the famous reference to ungulates and small spaces, or, to put it another way: "Then Jesus said to his disciples, 'Truly I tell you, it will be hard for a rich person to enter the kingdom of heaven. Again I tell you, it is easier for a camel to go through the eye of a needle than for someone who is rich to enter the kingdom of God.'" Jesus often speaks in hyperbole, and also insists in this and in other passages that everything is possible with God, but we can't simply dismiss or ignore what is being said here. Wealth is obviously a moral, practical, and spiritual problem and a direct hindrance to the Christian. Remember what comes before this statement and what has provoked Jesus's response:

> Then someone came to him and said, "Teacher, what good deed must I do to have eternal life?" And he said to him, "Why

> do you ask me about what is good? There is only one who is good. If you wish to enter into life, keep the commandments." He said to him, "Which ones?" And Jesus said, "You shall not murder; You shall not commit adultery; You shall not steal; You shall not bear false witness; Honour your father and mother; also, You shall love your neighbor as yourself." The young man said to him, "I have kept all these; what do I still lack?" Jesus said to him, "If you wish to be perfect, go, sell your possessions, and give the money to the poor, and you will have treasure in heaven; then come, follow me." When the young man heard this word, he went away grieving, for he had many possessions.

Matthew 6:24 has "No one can serve two masters; for a slave will either hate the one and love the other, or be devoted to the one and despise the other. You cannot serve God and wealth." St. Paul's First Letter to Timothy states, "But those who want to be rich fall into temptation and are trapped by many senseless and harmful desires that plunge people into ruin and destruction. For the love of money is a root of all kinds of evil, and in their eagerness to be rich some have wandered away from the faith and pierced themselves with many pains." The confrontation with the money changers occurs — unusually — in all four of the Gospels. "In the temple he found people selling cattle, sheep, and doves, and the money changers seated at their tables. Making a whip of cords, he drove all of them out of the temple. He also poured out the coins of the money changers and overturned their tables."

In all of these passages there is context, and the spiritual aspect always has to be understood first. In the temple, for example, those men behind their tables were likely selling bruised animals for sacrifice, thus betraying God. But they were also exploiting people, and while exchanging pagan coins for those permissible within holy ground, were doing so at inflated and dishonest prices. However one looks at this, and the other accounts of Jesus dealing with money and with those with great amounts of it, he is always deeply critical and suspicious. It's enough to make a capitalist blush, assuming they do such things.

In Matthew 25, we are told that Jesus said,

> "For I was hungry and you gave me food, I was thirsty and you gave me something to drink, I was a stranger and you welcomed me, I was naked and you gave me clothing, I was sick and you took care of me, I was in prison and you visited me." Then the righteous will answer him, "Lord, when was it that we saw you hungry and gave you food, or thirsty and gave you something to drink? And when was it that we saw you a stranger and welcomed you, or naked and gave you clothing? And when was it that we saw you sick or in prison and visited you?" And the king will answer them, "Truly I tell you, just as you did it to one of the least of these who are members of my family, you did it to me."

In this he is echoing the command initiated millennia earlier in the Old Testament: "The foreigner residing among you must be treated as your native-born. Love them as yourself, for you were foreigners in Egypt."

Consider the first letter of John:

> For this is the message you have heard from the beginning, that we should love one another. We must not be like Cain who was from the evil one and murdered his brother. And why did he murder him? Because his own deeds were evil and his brother's righteous. Do not be astonished, brothers and sisters, that the world hates you. We know that we have passed from death to life because we love one another. Whoever does not love abides in death. All who hate a brother or sister are murderers, and you know that murderers do not

> have eternal life abiding in them. We know love by this, that he laid down his life for us – and we ought to lay down our lives for one another. How does God's love abide in anyone who has the world's goods and sees a brother or sister in need and yet refuses help?

Then there is the letter of James:

> Come now, you rich people, weep and wail for the miseries that are coming to you. Your riches have rotted, and your clothes are moth-eaten. Your gold and silver have rusted, and their rust will be evidence against you, and it will eat your flesh like fire. You have laid up treasure for the last days. Listen! The wages of the laborers who mowed your fields, which you kept back by fraud, cry out, and the cries of the harvesters have reached the ears of the Lord of hosts. You have lived on the earth in luxury and in pleasure; you have fattened your hearts in a day of slaughter. You have condemned and murdered the righteous one, who does not resist you.

Some contemporary conservatives argue that while Jesus did indeed call for a redistribution of wealth, he envisaged this as charity, a voluntary act of generosity, and that these seemingly startling comments about wealth and ownership have to be read in the context of their era and culture. While context is always important, Jesus speaks about these issues so many times that they take on a significance far beyond mere contemporaneous commentary. There's also something of a double standard here, because these same doubters appear to have no such reservations when quoting what they believe to be strict biblical rules concerning sexuality and personal morality. The inescapable fact is that the Gospels are a revolutionary text, but the tenacity of political and religious escape artists never fails to surprise and impress me.

Let's look a little deeper. 1 Corinthians 12:25–26 has: "That there may be no dissension within the body, but the members may have the same care for one another. If one member suffers, all suffer together with it; if one member is honored, all rejoice together with it." 2 Corinthians 8:13–15 says, "I do not mean that there should be relief for others and pressure on you, but it is a question of a fair balance between your present abundance and their need, so that their abundance may be for your need, in order that there may be a fair balance. As it is written, 'The one who had much did not have too much, and the one who had little did not have too little.'"

Luke 14:33 tells us, "So therefore, none of you can become my disciple if you do not give up all your possessions." The book of Acts has: "Awe came upon everyone, because many wonders and signs were being done by the apostles. All who believed were together and had all things in common; they would sell their possessions and goods and distribute the proceeds to all, as any had need." And later, "Now the whole group of those who believed were of one heart and soul, and no one claimed private ownership of any possessions, but everything they owned was held in common. With great power the apostles gave their testimony to the resurrection of the Lord Jesus, and great grace was upon them all. There was not a needy person among them, for as many as owned lands or houses sold them and brought the proceeds of what was sold."

The Gospel of Matthew again: "Do not store up for yourselves treasures on earth, where moth and rust consume and where thieves break in and steal; but store up for yourselves treasures in heaven, where neither moth nor rust consumes and where thieves do not break in and steal. For where your treasure is, there your heart will be also." And the last segment of the Magnificat from Luke: "He has shown strength with his arm; he has scattered the proud in the thoughts of their hearts. He has brought down the powerful from their thrones, and lifted up the lowly; he has filled the hungry with good things, and sent the rich away empty."

Then we have the beatitudes. Do we seriously, honestly believe that they imply a conservative or a progressive spirit?

Blessed are the poor in spirit, for theirs is the kingdom of heaven.
Blessed are those who mourn, for they will be comforted.
Blessed are the meek, for they will inherit the earth.
Blessed are those who hunger and thirst for righteousness, for they will be filled.
Blessed are the merciful, for they will receive mercy.
Blessed are the pure in heart, for they will see God.
Blessed are the peacemakers, for they will be called children of God.
Blessed are those who are persecuted for righteousness' sake, for theirs is the kingdom of heaven.
Blessed are you when people revile you and persecute you and utter all kinds of evil against you falsely on my account.
Rejoice and be glad, for your reward is great in heaven, for in the same way they persecuted the prophets who were before you.

It's genuinely difficult to understand how anybody could interpret this as anything other than a revolutionary text, and as far as can be from a plea for complacency or conservatism. Even when Jesus performs the miracle of feeding a multitude of people with a limited amount of bread and fish, what we're seeing is either an extraordinary example of mass sharing and communal living, or a literal miracle where hungry people are fed. Either way, it's about fellowship, a joint effort, a coming-together of people who are hungry. Indeed, the New Testament is peppered with examples of the needy being fed and provided for. Remember Luke's Gospel — "Take care! Be on your guard against all kinds of greed; for one's life does not consist in the abundance of possessions." Take care, indeed.

When it comes to taxation, Jesus makes it somewhat difficult for those people today who employ accountants and financial advisers to "avoid" paying taxes, and thus failing to contribute to the general welfare of their fellow citizens. In Mark 12, we have the well-known reference to giving to Caesar what is his:

> Then they sent to him some Pharisees and some Herodians to trap him in what he said. And they came and said to him, "Teacher, we know that you are sincere, and show deference to no one; for you do not regard people with partiality, but teach the way of God in accordance with truth. Is it lawful to pay taxes to the emperor, or not? Should we pay them, or should we not?" But knowing their hypocrisy, he said to them, "Why are you putting me to the test? Bring me a denarius and let me see it." And they brought one. Then he said to them, "Whose head is this, and whose title?" They answered, "The emperor's." Jesus said to them, "Give to the emperor the things that are the emperor's, and to God the things that are God's." And they were utterly amazed at him.

There is much more going on here than a mere discussion about state-ordered redistribution of wealth — issues of pagan symbolism on coins, the separation of faith and government, and also the conflict between Jesus and the religious establishment of the time. Nevertheless, at no point does Jesus say anything about individual charity being the only way to help others. It's also simply too reductive and anachronistic to assume that all of the many calls of Christ for the poor, hungry, and needy to be helped have to be based on the potential and unpredictable largesse of the wealthy. Of course the state has a crucial place in Gospel-based attempts at economic and social equality. Taxation is also more efficient and more equitable than charity, as the history of the last hundred years has demonstrated countless times. It also helps to restore at least a small amount of balance to the enormous gaps in wealth that exist, often based on nothing more than what are often the fortunes, quite literally, of birth.

Speaking of taxes, in Luke 18:9–14 we read about those who regard themselves as superior, better, or part of the elite. The parable concerned those who revelled in their self-reliance, and regarded others with a certain contempt. Jesus says,

> Two men went up to the temple to pray, one a Pharisee and the other a tax collector. The Pharisee, standing by himself, was praying thus, "God, I thank you that I am not like other people: thieves, rogues, adulterers, or even like this tax collector. I fast twice a week; I give a tenth of all my income." But the tax collector, standing far off, would not even look up to heaven, but was beating his breast and saying, "God, be merciful to me, a sinner!" I tell you, this man went down to his home justified rather than the other; for all who exalt themselves will be humbled, but all who humble themselves will be exalted.

There's also a compelling juxtaposition involving health and healing that should be mentioned, which occurs in Mark 5:21–43. Jesus is approached by Jairus, a synagogue leader and obviously a man of some importance and stature. He falls at Jesus's feet and begs him, "My little daughter is at the point of death. Come and lay your hands on her, so that she may be made well, and live." Jesus agrees, but as he sets out a large crowd gathers around him, including a woman who had suffered from terrible bleeding for twelve years. Mark tells us that she had spent all of her money on numerous doctors but none had helped. She had become more and not less ill. She's heard stories about Jesus and his ability to heal, and touches his cloak. She is immediately healed. The rebel Christ may be surrounded by people but he knows that something has happened, and asked who was responsible. The poor woman, understandably frightened, comes forward to identify herself. Jesus reassures her: "Daughter, your faith has made you well; go in peace, and be healed of your disease."

A miracle, a sign of the supernatural power of the Son of God. But in the next paragraph, part of the same story, we see the synagogue leader told by some people from his house or place of work that his daughter had died, and that there is no point in wasting Jesus's time. "But overhearing what they said, Jesus said to the leader of the synagogue, 'Do not fear, only believe.'" They reach the house of the significant, influential man, and Jesus approaches the girl. "He took her by the hand and said to her, 'Talitha cum,' which means, 'Little girl, get up!' And immediately the girl got up and began to walk about (she was twelve years of age). At this they were overcome with amazement. He strictly ordered them that no one should know this, and told them to give her something to eat."

This passage concerns the miraculous, and the power of faith, but it also compares a poor woman, who had spent all of her money, with a child of privilege. The reaction of Jesus is not discrimination, not a preference of one over another, but a universal care and love. These people are equal in his sight, both deserving of concern and health, both worthy of life and healing.

While this book is about Jesus, we can't and mustn't ignore the Old Testament, the Hebrew Scriptures, which were — of course — the only holy books known and regarded by the Jewish people of the time, and also shaped the early church, both Jewish and gentile. The letters of St. Paul were the first parts of the New Testament to be written, and the first Gospel, that of Mark, wasn't written until around 70 CE. The Old Testament is, well, old. It's a complex and diverse set of books, written over many centuries, and it can be cherry-picked, often without context or full understanding, to try to prove all sorts of things — as we will see in the chapter on sexuality. That's an extremely dangerous and irresponsible approach to any analysis of an ancient text, but the idea of justice, economic and otherwise, runs through the writings like some divine thread of enlightenment, and a burning call for change and improvement. It's worth quoting from various different books to illustrate the point.

Jeremiah 2:34, says,

> On your skirts is found the lifeblood of the innocent poor, though you did not catch them breaking in. Yet in spite of all these things you say, "I am innocent; surely his anger has turned from me."

Isaiah tells us,

> Learn to do good; seek justice, rescue the oppressed, defend the orphan, plead for the widow.

And Psalm 82:

> Give justice to the weak and the orphan; maintain the right of the lowly and the destitute. Rescue the weak and the needy; deliver them from the hand of the wicked.

Deuteronomy 24:17–18:

> You shall not deprive a resident alien or an orphan of justice; you shall not take a widow's garment in pledge. Remember that you were a slave in Egypt and the Lord your God redeemed you from there; therefore I command you to do this.

And then:

> When you reap your harvest in your field, and forget a sheaf in the field, you shall not go back to get it; it shall be left for the alien, the orphan, and the widow, so that the Lord your God may bless you in all your undertakings. When you beat your olive trees, do not strip what is left; it shall be for the alien, the orphan, and the widow. When you gather the

> grapes of your vineyard, do not glean what is left; it shall be for the alien, the orphan, and the widow. Remember that you were a slave in the land of Egypt; therefore I am commanding you to do this.

Deuteronomy emphasizes economic justice, which is ironic because that is often used to justify conservative social policies. That's a profound misreading of the thrust of the book:

> If there is among you anyone in need, a member of your community in any of your towns within the land that the Lord your God is giving you, do not be hard-hearted or tight-fisted towards your needy neighbor. You should rather open your hand, willingly lending enough to meet the need, whatever it may be. Be careful that you do not entertain a mean thought, thinking, "The seventh year, the year of remission, is near," and therefore view your needy neighbour with hostility and give nothing; your neighbour might cry to the Lord against you, and you would incur guilt. Give liberally and be ungrudging when you do so, for on this account the Lord your God will bless you in all your work and in all that you undertake. Since there will never cease to be some in need on the earth, I therefore command you, "Open your hand to the poor and needy neighbor in your land."

And:

> You shall not withhold the wages of poor and needy laborers, whether other Israelites or aliens who reside in your land in one of your towns. You shall pay them their wages daily before sunset, because they are poor and their livelihood depends on them; otherwise they might cry to the Lord against you, and you would incur guilt.

Leviticus, another Old Testament book often used by those on the right of the political spectrum, insists in 25:35, "If any of your kin fall into difficulty and become dependent on you, you shall support them; they shall live with you as though resident aliens. Do not take interest in advance or otherwise make a profit from them, but fear your God; let them live with you." And Amos instructs in 5:14, "Seek good and not evil, that you may live; and so the Lord, the God of hosts, will be with you, just as you have said. Hate evil and love good, and establish justice in the gate; it may be that the Lord, the God of hosts, will be gracious to the remnant of Joseph."

So whose side is Jesus on? That's too linear and simple a question, of course, but it's worth asking if we're to counter the claim, almost considered self-evident by some, that he's somehow standing in and with the ranks of the powerful, the dominant, the reactionary, and the legalistic. This is crucial, because far too many within conservative Christianity have fallen into the trap of not wanting to become more like Jesus, but of wanting Jesus to become more like them. Rather than building their morality around Christ, they build Christ around their morality. So it's Jesus the Republican, Jesus the Tory, Jesus the warrior, Jesus the Pharisee. Yes, Jesus the Pharisee. The very people who most relentlessly opposed him, the purists and pedants of the time, seem to have won the battle for religion in far too many twent-first-century churches. Over and over again in the Gospels, we see Jesus being tested by legalists who try to expose him as being unreliable and heretical. Whether he is healing people, or instructing us on how to observe the fast, or even when the controversy concerns the men and women with whom he associates — often not the "right sort of people at all!" — he presents a startlingly different model of how we should live and behave.

The following passage is used a lot, but it's always worth remembering, and considering in full. The Gospel of John:

> The scribes and the Pharisees brought a woman who had been caught in adultery; and making her stand before all of

> them, they said to him, "Teacher, this woman was caught in the very act of committing adultery. Now in the law Moses commanded us to stone such women. Now what do you say?" They said this to test him, so that they might have some charge to bring against him. Jesus bent down and wrote with his finger on the ground. When they kept on questioning him, he straightened up and said to them, "Let anyone among you who is without sin be the first to throw a stone at her." And once again he bent down and wrote on the ground. When they heard it, they went away, one by one, beginning with the elders; and Jesus was left alone with the woman standing before him. Jesus straightened up and said to her, "Woman, where are they? Has no one condemned you?" She said, "No one, sir." And Jesus said, "Neither do I condemn you. Go your way, and from now on do not sin again."

This story may not have been in the original text, and might not be by John at all, but it certainly influenced Christians from very early on in the church's history. The Greek wording is also slightly ambiguous, and Jesus may have been drawing rather than writing, but if he was indeed writing in the sand it was likely something along the lines of "Stop constantly trying to twist my words and actions, you guys!" So, what does this poignant and memorable scene tell us about the nature of Jesus and the faith that he left for us?

Surely the answer is that empathy and understanding are more important than anything else, and that in our rush to judge and to single out "the other" we lose all sense of what it is to be in a relationship with God, and with the divine plan for human behaviour and happiness. The wonderful, wise Christian author and columnist Rachel Held Evans, who was taken from us far too young when she died in 2019 at just thirty-seven years old, wrote this about what happened that day in the small, dusty town in the Middle East:

> He knew that hers would be invisible stones, the kind she'd grip tighter each time she saw the man who once shared her bed but not her public humiliation, each time she heard the whispers of her neighbors or the loud, pretentious prayers of the men who had grabbed her and surrounded her and threatened to kill her, each time she heard rumors that the person who saved her would himself be put to death.
>
> She would sin, no doubt.
>
> But perhaps she would think twice before casting those stones. Perhaps she would stop for a moment to consider the irony of becoming just like her accusers.
>
> We tend to look down our noses at these ancient people with their purity codes regulating everything from the fibers in their clothes to the people they touched. But we have our own purity codes these days – people we cast out from our communities or surround with Bible-wielding mobs, labels we assign to those who don't fit, conditions we place on God's grace, theological and behavioral checklists we hand out before baptism or communion, sins real or imagined we delight in taking seriously because we'd like to think they are much more severe than our own.

Yes, yes, yes! Different moral codes today, different ideas of what constitutes being unacceptable, but still the stigma and the judgment.

This is a story about a man named Horse. Not the movie, just a man. An odd name, but his own. I met him when he had fallen on very hard times, indeed. When we were first introduced we had coffee and breakfast and I asked him, not unreasonably, how he had got his name. He told me that it was "Jack" really, but that everybody called him Horse because of something very deep and personal. I asked him what. "I was married, and we had a little girl. Julie," he explained. "We came to the big city from a small town, lots of work around. I did some building, some demolition. We were okay. Julie liked school, my wife and I were having a good time." More confident now, the words flowing.

"Yes, we drank a little, but never in front of the girl. I wasn't a drunk, never! Then the marriage came apart. Maybe it was me, maybe it was her. She said I wasn't ambitious. I worked hard, but was getting nowhere. I looked for work, did anything, anything. But then she found this other guy. Can't blame her really, he had a lot more to offer her. She left me. Left Julie too. So, there we were. But we had each other, had a small apartment. She liked life, had clothes and friends, and I tell you, no dad loved a daughter as much as I did her. But then she got these headaches. Went to the doc, he said they'd go. They didn't. Got worse. Then one night she screamed, and I called the ambulance." He pauses, puts his hands inside his coat for a few moments as if to hold something. "They got her to the hospital but I think she was already gone by then. I'm sure they tried their best, but they kept looking at me in a funny away, like it was my fault somehow. It wasn't. It really wasn't." He looks down, unable to continue.

I felt tearful, moved, unable and powerless to do anything other than listen. Then, after we steady ourselves, I ask the obvious question. But why do they call you Horse? In explanation he pulls a child's tiny toy horse from out of his greasy, long-worn coat. "It belonged to her, you see. She was holding it when she died. It was still warm from her little hand. She wouldn't let go of it. It's all I have left. Can't let go, can't let go. I hold it next to my heart. The other guys know I have it, so they call me Horse."

The other guys were those who had also fallen on hard times, lived in hostels or even on the street. Horse had found his way out of the life, with help from others, and eventually by a circuitous route had become a Christian, a friend of the rebel Christ. Problem was, the first couple of churches he attended didn't seem to want him. He sometimes went along after a Saturday night on a bench, didn't always look the part, hadn't shaved in a while. The other churchgoers made their lack of ease rather apparent, and so he moved on. Eventually, he found a church that not only embraced him but made him part of their family. But before then he had been judged and found wanting. He had been outside of the narrow code, that broadband of legalism, that decided who is deserving of acceptance, and who should be considered stained, wrong, and sinful. Who, perhaps, should have symbolic stones thrown at them.

Now consider the modern equivalent of Jesus and the woman being condemned, and the people around them shouting their condemnation. Who comes to mind, what images burn into the psyche, how does it make us feel? That woman in the centre of the circle of abuse and marginalization is the refugee, the asylum seeker, the trans person, the street kid, the drug user, the sex worker, the slum dweller, the different, the not-like-us, the easy-to-reject-and-ignore. Oh, how satisfying it is, how smug it makes us feel, to point at them so as to reassure ourselves that we're not like that. We all do it. I do it. But he didn't.

That is the rebel who was Jesus, who was the Christ.

He was also someone who hated and rejected violence. I don't happen to think that the Christian faith demands that we be pacifist, and I believe that there are occasions — though very few of them — when an armed and cruel oppressor has to be resisted by force. It is one thing for us as individuals to embrace nonresistance, but perhaps a different matter when another person, other people, or an entire race face sadistic exploitation or even genocidal slaughter. Even in such cases, war and violence are often avoidable if other steps are taken, and in the oft-quoted case of the Second World War and the righteous struggles against Nazism, so much could have been done so much earlier to prevent the rise of Hitlerism, and to employ moral and diplomatic force against than incalculable evil. It's a matter open to debate, but I for one won't make blanket statements about absolute pacifism. What we can say is that Jesus was as far from a warlord or a man of violence as it's possible to be. For example, from Matthew:

"Blessed are the peacemakers, for they will be called children of God" and "You have heard that it was said, 'An eye for an eye and a tooth for a tooth.' But I say to you, Do not resist an evildoer. But if anyone strikes you on the right cheek, turn the other also." And "Put your sword back into its place; for all who take the sword will perish by the sword." And from Luke, "But I say to you that listen, Love your enemies, do good to those who hate you, bless those who curse you, pray for those who abuse you." And in Matthew's Gospel, "See, I am sending you out like sheep into the midst of wolves; so be wise as serpents and innocent as doves."

One of the most effective and respected Christians of the twentieth century, Martin Luther King Jr., seems so diametrically opposed to many of today's public believers on a number of pressing issues. He said that violence was, paradoxically, weak and ineffective. It's "a descending spiral, begetting the very thing it seeks to destroy." Rather than combatting what is opposed, it makes it ever more powerful. "Through violence you murder the hater, but you do not murder hate.... Returning violence for violence multiplies violence, adding deeper darkness to a night already devoid of stars. Darkness cannot drive out darkness; only light can do that. Hate cannot drive out hate; only love can do that."

When St. Paul discusses the issue, he is often speaking of the church itself, and how church members should behave to one another. But surely if this is how Christians are supposed to act within their own communities, they can't and won't suddenly change their attitudes when interacting with those outside of the church — especially as they are required to be daily witnesses to their faith, and to the teachings of Jesus. The letter to the Colossians says:

> As God's chosen ones, holy and beloved, clothe yourselves with compassion, kindness, humility, meekness, and patience. Bear with one another and, if anyone has a complaint against another, forgive each other; just as the Lord has forgiven you,

> so you also must forgive. Above all, clothe yourselves with love, which binds everything together in perfect harmony. And let the peace of Christ rule in your hearts, to which indeed you were called in the one body. And be thankful. Let the word of Christ dwell in you richly; teach and admonish one another in all wisdom; and with gratitude in your hearts sing psalms, hymns, and spiritual songs to God. And whatever you do, in word or deed, do everything in the name of the Lord Jesus, giving thanks to God the Father through him.

In his letter to the Romans, Paul writes that we should not repay evil with evil and that, if at all possible, should live in peace with everybody, and that we should overcome evil with good. St. Peter says we should not "repay evil for evil or abuse for abuse; but, on the contrary, repay with a blessing. It is for this that you were called — that you might inherit a blessing."

The Old Testament speaks of many wars, of acts of violence, and it records the history of a people who by no means always lived lives of peace and tranquility. It would be too convenient, and somewhat facile, to simply declare the Hebrew Scriptures a narrative of non-violence. But there is, as always, context, historical record, and desired purpose; what do we do, and what should we do. The book of Micah has: "He shall judge between many peoples, and shall arbitrate between strong nations far away; they shall beat their swords into plowshares, and their spears into pruning hooks; nation shall not lift up sword against nation, neither shall they learn war anymore."

And something many of us might hear sung, or even sing ourselves, at Christmas but not give it very much consideration, from Isaiah 9:6–7: "For a child has been born for us, a son given to us; authority rests upon his shoulders; and he is named Wonderful Counselor, Mighty God, Everlasting Father, Prince of Peace. His authority shall grow continually, and there shall be endless peace for the throne of David and his kingdom. He will establish and uphold it with justice and with righteousness from this time onward and forevermore. The zeal of the Lord of hosts will do this."

When Jesus speaks of war and peace, he uses words that, in the ancient Greek version, are not passive and soft but aggressively interventionist, strident against violence, and militant in bringing about peace. At heart he is telling listeners that if they make war, or even allow war to take place without doing all in their power to prevent it, they don't know God. Jesus is less a pacifist — witness the attack on the money men in the temple — than a committed objector to war. No selling arms, no military-industrial complex, no profit in other people's misery. Yet the amount of money spent on the military has increased by 75 percent over the past twenty years and is now around $1.8 trillion. By any standards that is a quite breathtaking amount, but when we remember that is spent directly on weapons of destruction, on increasingly deadly and efficient methods to wound and kill people, it is positively obscene. Much of it, God forgive us, is spent by countries that are nominally Christian, led by people who claim to be followers of Christ.

Jesus was about human dignity. He taught that all of humanity was created in precious equality. That equality includes those who were unlucky enough to have been born in countries that have suffered through war, exploitation, colonization, or poverty, sometimes caused directly by wealthy countries claiming to be Christian. National borders are made by people, but people are made by God. Yet immigration is often feared and resisted, and refugees seen as a problem rather than a blessing. We witnessed some of this at its most severe when the Donald Trump administration separated families at the U.S. border, put children in cages, and expunged the very humanity of people who were merely trying to escape poverty and danger. Yet former President Trump's actions were applauded by tens of millions of active and committed Christians. And while Trump's actions were outstandingly egregious, other presidents and other world leaders who consider themselves to be Christian have performed little better. The rebel Christ would have us act differently.

In the Hebrew Scriptures the words *gûr* and *gēr* are usually translated as "stranger" but can also mean "alien" or "newcomer." In the first five books of the Old Testament, what we know of as the Pentateuch, the word is found close to fifty times, and the references are fascinating and revealing. Deuteronomy tells us,

> For the Lord your God is God of gods and Lord of lords, the great God, mighty and awesome, who is not partial and takes no bribe, who executes justice for the orphan and the widow, and who loves the strangers, providing them food and clothing. You shall also love the stranger, for you were strangers in the land of Egypt.

And:

> When you have finished paying all the tithe of your produce in the third year (which is the year of the tithe), giving it to the Levites, the aliens, the orphans, and the widows, so that they may eat their fill within your towns, then you shall say before the Lord your God: "I have removed the sacred portion from the house, and I have given it to the Levites, the resident aliens, the orphans, and the widows, in accordance with your entire commandment that you commanded me."

The second passage goes further than demanding a love of the stranger, but tells us to actively support them with what we have worked to produce. This is not some passive call for decency and civility but a firm and formed plan to aid the aliens — strangers or newcomers — when they enter our lands. Jeremiah, in warning people that there would be dire consequences if they disobeyed God's plan, tells those who claim to follow the truth, "For if you truly amend your ways and your doings, if you truly act justly one with another, if you do not oppress the alien, the orphan, and the widow, or shed innocent blood in this place, and if you do not go after other gods to your own hurt, then I will dwell with you in this place, in the land that I gave of old to your ancestors forever and ever." That's a very long way from putting children in cages, separating families, and insulting refugees by calling them rapists and killers.

In the New Testament, in the Gospel of Matthew, Jesus says that when the time comes, "All the nations will be gathered" and that there will be judgment according to how people acted. Some will be found to have acted according to God's will because "I was hungry and you gave me food, I was thirsty and you gave me something to drink, I was a stranger and you welcomed me, I was naked and you gave me clothing, I was sick and you took care of me, I was in prison and you visited me." When Jesus is asked how that can be because the listeners never saw him hungry, thirsty, or as a stranger, he replies, "Truly I tell you, just as you did it to one of the least of these who are members of my family, you did it to me," and, more chillingly, of those who refused to help: "I was a stranger and you did not welcome me, naked and you did not give me clothing, sick and in prison and you did not visit me." Their fate is made clear. "Truly I tell you, just as you did not do it to one of the least of these, you did not do it to me. And these will go away into eternal punishment, but the righteous into eternal life."

That, one would think and hope, would reshape any anti-immigration ideas that Christians might hold, but apparently a great many seem to have more faith in strict border controls than they do in the word of their saviour. The command to love one's neighbour as oneself — the very quintessence of Christianity — can't really be disputed by anybody with even a passing knowledge of Jesus. It becomes particularly pertinent to this issue as many scholars and linguists believe that "neighbour" and "stranger" (also meaning "newcomer" or, in modern terms, "immigrant") are essentially the same thing. Love the immigrant, says the rebel Christ. Love the immigrant as yourself.

In Paul's letter to the Galatians he writes that "there is no longer Jew or Greek, there is no longer slave or free, there is no longer male and female; for all of you are one in Christ Jesus," and throughout Scripture the thrust is toward shared humanity rather than the separating and dividing of people, culminating in the unity that is Jesus.

That unity demands an opposition to racism, which continues to be a sin screaming out for repair. This is something that became particularly obvious during the height of the latest wave of demonstrations for racial justice that began in 2020 — after centuries of suffering — but continue and, God willing, will continue until we have fully dealt with the sin of racism and its murderous consequences. For Christians, this was directly relevant for numerous and, I'd hope, obvious reasons. The church has so often failed when it comes to race, too often even led that hideous failure. It has been on the side of the reaction, not the rebellion.

In the midst of these entirely laudable reactions — these protests and rallies — to racial injustice and police brutality, incidents of spontaneous iconoclasm occurred. Statues of notorious slavers and Confederate leaders were toppled and the damned things should never have been there in the first place. There were also calls to remove statues, pictures, and icons that were less obviously offensive, and demands by a minority of activists to remove or destroy depictions of "white Jesus" and his white family. This brought, and brings, to the surface an extremely important aspect of the authentic Jesus, and one that is central in the search for the rebel we claim to know.

The truth, of course, is that Yeshua and his people were first-century Middle Eastern Jews, and while there was a certain variety of looks because of the mixed composition of the Mosaic exodus, most would have been dark-skinned and certainly not the Scandinavian Messiah so readily and inaccurately depicted in churches. Is it relevant? Surely, Jesus's appearance matters far less than what he did and taught.

Problem is, the obsession with the iconography of a white Jesus has so infected the faith historically, and continues to do so even today, that Christians have felt enabled to treat people of colour appallingly.

This has been most keenly seen in Christianity's relationship with slavery. Few churches have clean records regarding the obscenity; as early as the fifteenth century, the Roman Catholic Church gave its official endorsement in a set of papal bulls. In the years before the U.S. Civil War, the church was one of the largest slave-owning entities in four states, and in South America, various religious orders enslaved countless men and women, working them to enormous profit. The Church of England was an integral part of the emerging empire and did much to develop and institutionalize the transatlantic slave trade. When the British 1833 Slavery Abolition Act was passed, paying out £20 million ($33.8 million) to slave owners across the British Empire, many of those who received this "compensation" were Anglican clergy.

The Methodists were nobler, with founder John Wesley denouncing slavery as "the sum of all villainies." Various nonconformist Christians outside of the mainstream were similarly convinced. As a church, the Quakers were probably the most vehement in standing against the evil of human ownership. And the Christian abolitionist movement, which produced heroic figures such as William Wilberforce and Thomas Clarkson in the late eighteenth and early nineteenth centuries, was extraordinary in its courage and determination.

But this is the point, really. The abolitionists were extraordinary when they should have been ordinary. Their spirit should have been commonplace within organized Christianity, and it wasn't. They should have been some of countless, but they weren't. Wilberforce and his followers were often opposed by other Christians, and those who weren't actively against them were often indifferent, or disguised their apathy with excuses. In this case the cry was "If Britain abolishes slavery, the French will take it over. Or the Spanish, the Dutch, or Portuguese. Let us consider all of this later." It's chilling how eerily similar this sounds to those contemporary complainers who reject policies to counter climate change.

Christians also struggled to end U.S. slavery in the nineteenth century, but other committed believers led the Confederacy, and continued to regret the loss of slavery, and to embrace racism. It's a painfully disarming story, and the fact that so many Africans and people of African heritage remain faithful Christians is a tribute to their ability to see the authentic Jesus, the rebel Christ, through all of the racist distortion, and to their invincible grace to forgive.

The Bible itself is at best ambiguous. The Old Testament writes of slavery, often without censure and even with approval. As such, it describes a society that differs little from many of the other slave-based cultures of the ancient world. The New Testament may not be as absolute, but the few specific references to slavery are far from encouraging. Over the centuries, churches have evolved and matured, with Christian institutions often confessing the darker sides of their histories. But it would be disingenuous to argue that the present is not somehow a product of the past. Former archbishop of Canterbury Rowan Williams put it well: "The Body of Christ is not just a body that exists at any one time; it exists across history and we therefore share the shame and the sinfulness of our predecessors." Ultimately, this shouldn't be some morbid attempt at historical justification, but rather an opportunity to move forward with full disclosure and crisp transparency. Christians should be in a condition of permanent revolution and embrace the constant admission that we can be better and do more.

But where does the rebel Christ come into the equation? I'd respond by asking another question. When we read the Gospels, when we study the life, character, and teachings of Jesus, can we envisage someone who would have tolerated slavery, and who would remain silent in the face of racism and human degradation? Everything we know about him would make that impossible. Christians need to be completely honest about the past, and also completely honest about the man they worship. Jesus isn't the establishment, Jesus is the outsider. Jesus isn't the powerful, Jesus is the powerless. Jesus isn't the slaver, Jesus is the slave.

Sometimes the Christian ability to miss the point of the whole thing can be as absurd as it is frustrating. In 2017, for example, the British bakery Greggs was obliged to apologize after it produced an ad depicting a nativity scene with the assorted worshippers praising not the baby Messiah but a sausage roll. It was part of the company's Advent calendar, entitled — with a splendidly eponymous leap of imagination — "Merry Greggsmas." One of the first things Christians are taught in catechism class should be that the Son of God is not a sausage roll. Other pastry snacks are not specified, but he is never, ever a sausage roll.

Little did the good people at Greggs realize what an uproar this would cause, with the extraordinarily powerful British tabloid press joining forces with various conservative Christians to denounce yet another example of the ongoing "war on Christmas." But here, reality cries out to be heard: This was merely a slightly insensitive and crass campaign to sell meat products. More than this, there is not and never has been a war on Christmas, whether it's the appearance of Happy Holidays cards (so what?), multicultural television commercials (surely a good thing), or carol singers allegedly being banned from shopping malls (they aren't). But the sausage roll reveals a sorry irony. If there is a religious war, it is not on the season we have somewhat arbitrarily and relatively recently chosen as the date of Jesus's birth. Rather, it is an attack against the Christian, egalitarian virtues that the child and the event are supposed to epitomize — a charge led by some Christians and churches themselves.

But if anything should anger followers of Jesus at Christmas, or any other time, it shouldn't be some irrelevant commercial for food, but rather the fact that millions of people go without food altogether; it shouldn't be that Jesus's name is taken in vain but that his teachings are taken in vain; it shouldn't be that we don't say "Merry Christmas" as often as we did, but that we so seldom say "I forgive you," "You are loved," and "All are welcome in church." After all, per the once-ubiquitous question "What would Jesus do," the answer would probably be "tell everyone to grow up, reread what the New Testament says, and then go and turn the world upside down" — not just at Christmas, but every day of the year.

Thing is, none of this is about ideological socialism, or being especially or dramatically on the political left, at least in party terms. It's about being a Christian. Historically, many people who have regarded themselves as being conservative have embraced the Christian message and in doing so changed the entire world. The late eighteenth century British MP William Wilberforce wasn't affiliated to a party as such but he was certainly allied to conservatives and had conservative views on all sorts of subjects. Yet he led the campaign against slavery and devoted his life to that cause. Anthony Ashley-Cooper, seventh Earl of Shaftesbury, was a nineteenth-century Tory MP in the British parliament and a strong supporter of the extremely conservative Duke of Wellington. Yet his Christian faith led him to work tirelessly to reform conditions for the mentally ill, and for working people, especially children, in factories and other workplaces. "Social reforms, so necessary, so indispensable, require as much of God's grace as a change of heart," he said, as he campaigned to improve education, health care, and welfare for those so long neglected. Conservatism needn't be muddied in the Christian nationalism and disturbed literalism that we see so often bruising the public face of the modern church.

Consider, of all people, television's Mr. Rogers. What is fascinating to realize in this age of right-wing evangelicalism is that Mr. Rogers was a lifelong Republican. He opposed former president Richard Nixon on many issues, he was consistently progressive on racial equality, and embraced many liberal virtues, but was nevertheless a Republican and considered himself a conservative. We might regard him as a saccharine lightweight, but since his death in 2003 a new realization has occurred of just how influential, and beneficial, he was not just to American children, but also to the country's perception and understanding of itself, especially at a time when self-doubt and even self-loathing are so prominent. Fred Rogers, he of puppets, toys, and perennial optimism, is seen as the best of America. But that is rather missing the point.

The quintessence of the man was not his nationality but his faith. If he was the best of anything, it was Christianity, which stuns those who are understandably cut and hurt by a faith that in the United States is often seen now as intolerant, and as infecting rather than informing the body politic. With Mr. Rogers, the faith was implicit, and it was this subtle witness of grace that made him so compelling. He's not the only Christian in public life to have acted thus, of course, but this is where the difficulty, the paradox, presents itself. As we've seen, far too often, the loudest of believers are those on the raucous right, who instead of speaking of the good news shout about the bad.

He was a Presbyterian, and an ordained minister, but rather than fierce Calvinism, his theology was bathed in optimism. "The big thing about God is God's faithfulness: not giving up on those with whom God has made covenant," he said. And, "I'm wary of people who insist on trying to make other people feel bad about themselves. The more I look around me and within me, the more I notice that those who feel best about themselves have the greatest capacity to feel good about others." So, when we see him gently prodding us, adults as well as children, toward something universal and — in its purest, most authentic form — kind, we're not witnessing banality but heartfelt belief. He once told an angry Christian who insisted that people were damned unless they found Jesus, "God loves you just the way you are." That tension was epitomized by his relationship with François Clemmons, an African American actor whom he brought into the show to play a police officer, at a time when Black performers were seldom seen on television shows for children. Clemmons was also gay, and while he says that Mr. Rogers was affirming of his sexuality, he also told him off-screen not to attend gay clubs in case he was noticed and thus offended valuable sponsors. Yet, in one particularly poignant episode of the show in 1969, set on a hot summer day, Mr. Rogers asks Mr. Clemmons to cool his feet in the water of a paddling pool, and after Mr. Clemmons dries his feet, Mr. Rogers uses the same towel to dry his own. This was at a time when large parts of the United States were still segregated, and only months after the assassination of Martin Luther King Jr. Here was Fred Rogers, a hero for children and an icon to adults, sharing a towel with a Black gay man. The Christian symbolism is inescapable. It took a children's entertainer to appreciate that, to live it, and to introduce it as a conservative and a Republican to the neighbourhood.

Labels are rarely helpful and often damaging, and there can be an anger and intolerance on the left that shames the name of equality and progress. Also, if Christianity is centred on forgiveness as well as social justice, we have to provide people with an opportunity as well as a reason to change and transform. As I wrote earlier, I don't come from a Christian family, and my father's people were Russian Jews. While most left for Britain in the 1890s, some remained behind and a great-uncle fought in the Red Army through most of the Second World War. I met him only once, when I was a child. He wore his uniform for the reunion, drank vodka all day, and pinched my cheek a lot. It hurt. "There are two types of vodka, Michaela," he said. "Good vodka, and very good vodka." Because he spoke Yiddish, he was used as an interpreter by the Soviet army when German soldiers were interrogated, and sometimes their lives were in his hands. He was reluctant to say much about his experiences, but did tell us about a teenager his unit captured in 1945. The boy admitted to being in the SS, he cried, and he begged. My uncle's commander asked what he was saying. "He's a kid who has been digging tunnels for them," uncle replied. "He's nothing." They let him live.

I asked why he had done that, especially when the Nazis had murdered some of his relatives. In broken English and with his perennial smile briefly gone, he replied, "I'd seen enough." Then a pause. "Sometimes we have to forgive, sometimes we have to forgive." I'm not sure I could have been as strong as that, but as a Christian, forgiveness is at the very heart of what I am called to embrace. I have to forgive because I have been forgiven, and that should be a constant and defining feature of the Christian life.

As I said in the introduction to this book, this isn't about political parties or even ideologies. It's about the blistering calls for change and justice that permeate the Jesus story, a story that never changes, even if we sometimes misplace its meaning. And about following that story not with hubris but with humility, always peppering our confidence in the truth with a commitment to empathy and forgiveness.

Chapter 3

God Made People Gay, He Didn't Make Them Gay-Hating

Back in 1978, Britain's highly successful and influential Tom Robinson Band released the song "(Sing if You're) Glad to Be Gay." It became, understandably, something of an anthem in the LGBTQ2 community but for some reason never caught on in the church music scene. Yes, that's supposed to be amusing. Having said that, today in many churches in the western world, rainbow flags are waved, and Christians have come to their senses about the issue. But among conservatives in North America and Europe, and in particular in large parts of Africa, the Caribbean, the Middle East, and Eastern Europe, homosexuality remains a virtual obsession, seen as a sin of sins. The pain and destruction this approach causes is, needless to say, beyond calculation. Such homophobia is deadly. I use that word advisedly. It genuinely leads to people being killed.

I want to spend quite a bit of time and space on the subject here because in so many ways it typifies the problem faced by the modern church — confusion over what Scripture actually means, the gripping of one or two particular subjects as a way to provide a cause and justification for certain actions and attitudes, and the abandonment of the most crucial aspect of the rebel Christ — the call to love and to accept. But what you'll realize in this chapter is that we quote Jesus less than elsewhere in the book, and other biblical writers more. The reason is that Jesus doesn't explicitly mention the subject at all. Yet because conservative Christians are so concerned with homosexuality, the arguments have to be countered if the true Christ and his church are to be explained and defended, and that demands references to the Old Testament and to the Pauline letters.

The obsession in itself is strange for many reasons, especially in that there are probably a mere five or six mentions of what can loosely be described as homosexuality in the entire Bible. Malcolm Johnson exposes this bewildering perversion of emphasis rather well in his book, *Diary of a Gay Priest: The Tightrope Walker*: "It is condemned. It is expressly forbidden in Scripture … Four General Councils forbid it, Luther and Zwingli weighed against it, and until recently it was distasteful to most people. What is it? Lending money at interest." In fact only a tiny fraction of the Bible is in any way related to same-sex relationships whereas more than 10 percent is devoted to issues of economic inequality, exploitation, and injustice, indicated by what we saw in the last chapter. From a literalist point of view, then, conservatives are looking through the wrong end of the theological telescope and seeing the important themes as distant, blurred, black-and-white images and the insignificant on seventy-inch colour plasma screens.

On a less sophisticated but deliciously naughty level there is a letter that has been doing the social media rounds for a few years now that was written by someone — we're still not precisely sure who the original culprit was — in response to the extremely conservative and ostentatiously religious Dr. Laura Schlessinger, who seems to have rather faded away these days. It may seem a little surprising to speak of the notorious radio host in a book about the reality of Christ, but I think this example sums up the disconnect between perception and fact rather well. The alleged expert had repeatedly made negative remarks about homosexuality, same-sex relationships, and equal marriage, and based much of what she said on biblical precedent. She went so far as to refer to gays as "mistakes of nature" and at her peak spoke to an enormous and eager audience. She is not, by the way, a medical doctor.

> Dear Dr. Laura: Thank you for doing so much to educate people regarding God's Law. I have learned a great deal from your show, and try to share that knowledge with as many people as I can. When someone tries to defend the homosexual lifestyle, for example, I simply remind them that Leviticus 18:22 clearly states it to be an abomination ... end of debate. I do need some advice from you, however, regarding some other elements of God's Laws and how to follow them.
>
> 1) Leviticus 25:44 states that I may possess slaves, both male and female, provided they are purchased from neighbouring nations. A friend of mine claims that this applies to Mexicans, but not Canadians. Can you clarify? Why can't I own Canadians?
>
> 2) I would like to sell my daughter into slavery, as sanctioned in Exodus 21:7. In this day and age, what do you think would be a fair price for her?
>
> 3) I know that I am allowed no contact with a woman while she is in her period of menstrual unseemliness – Lev. 15:19-24. The problem is how do I tell? I have tried asking, but most women take offence.
>
> 4) When I burn a bull on the altar as a sacrifice, I know it creates a pleasing odor for the Lord – Lev. 1:9. The problem is my neighbours. They claim the odor is not pleasing to them. Should I smite them?
>
> 5) I have a neighbour who insists on working on the Sabbath. Exodus 35:2 clearly states he should be put to

death. Am I morally obligated to kill him myself, or should I ask the police to do it?

6) A friend of mine feels that even though eating shellfish is an abomination, Lev. 11:10, it is a lesser abomination than homosexuality. I don't agree. Can you settle this? Are there "degrees" of abomination?

7) Lev. 21:20 states that I may not approach the altar of God if I have a defect in my sight. I have to admit that I wear reading glasses. Does my vision have to be 20/20, or is there some wiggle-room here?

8) Most of my male friends get their hair trimmed, including the hair around their temples, even though this is expressly forbidden by Lev. 19:27. How should they die?

9) I know from Lev. 11:6–8 that touching the skin of a dead pig makes me unclean, but may I still play football if I wear gloves?

10) My uncle has a farm. He violates Lev. 19:19 by planting two different crops in the same field, as does his wife by wearing garments made of two different kinds of thread (cotton/polyester blend). He also tends to curse and blaspheme a lot. Is it really necessary that we go to all the trouble of getting the whole town together to stone them? Lev. 24:10–16. Couldn't we just burn them to death at a private family affair, like we do with people who sleep with their in-laws? (Lev. 20:14)

I know you have studied these things extensively and thus enjoy considerable expertise in such matters, so I am confident you can help. Thank you again for reminding us that God's word is eternal and unchanging.

Delightful stuff.

One of the ironies, one of the imploding paradoxes of all this, is that the more fundamentalist and literalist that Christians become the more they disagree about who has the correct understanding of Scripture. Taking the Bible as literal truth, without need of context and interpretation, doesn't unite Christians but achieves the very opposite. In the 1980s, the American stand-up comic Emo Philips wrote a joke that still hits at the heart of truth.

> Once I saw this guy on a bridge about to jump. I said, "Don't do it!"
>
> He said, "Nobody loves me."
>
> I said, "God loves you. Do you believe in God?"
>
> He said, "Yes."
>
> I said, "Are you a Christian or a Jew?"
>
> He said, "A Christian."
>
> I said, "Me, too! Protestant or Catholic?"
>
> He said, "Protestant."
>
> I said, "Me, too! What franchise?"
>
> He said, "Baptist."
>
> I said, "Me, too! Northern Baptist or Southern Baptist?"
>
> He said, "Northern Baptist."
>
> I said, "Me, too! Northern Conservative Baptist or Northern Liberal Baptist?"
>
> He said, "Northern Conservative Baptist."
>
> I said, "Me, too! Northern Conservative Baptist Great Lakes Region, or Northern Conservative Baptist Eastern Region?"
>
> He said, "Northern Conservative Baptist Great Lakes Region."
>
> I said, "Me, too! Northern Conservative Baptist Great Lakes Region Council of 1879, or Northern Conservative Baptist Great Lakes Region Council of 1912?"
>
> He said, "Northern Conservative Baptist Great Lakes Region Council of 1912."
>
> I said, "Die, heretic!" And I pushed him over.

Which is where you're supposed to laugh. Or not.

The Christian understanding of the Bible, and opinions on how to live and implement biblical teachings, also change with the times. If this sounds too convenient to the subject we're discussing, we only have to apply it to any number of historical or even recent examples of church beliefs. Take perhaps the most viscerally troubling subject, that of slavery. It has always existed in human history in various forms but the European, white enslavement of enormous numbers of men and women from Africa began in the sixteenth century and reached a highly lucrative and obscene peak in the eighteenth and first half of the nineteenth centuries. The abolitionist movement was led by Christians, usually evangelical and Quaker, and we cannot fully understand the work of William Wilberforce, Thomas Clarkson, John Newton, and the rest without realizing that they were motivated and mobilized by a powerful Christian revulsion at slavery based on their reading of the Bible. Without Christian men and women moved to passion and anger by the sin of slavery the trade would have continued for far longer. But while many of the defenders of slavery were unconcerned with religion and were driven by profit or indifference there were many in the pro-slavery camp who were Bible-believing Christians and felt justified in their defence of the indefensible by their approach to Scripture.

They pointed to Abraham's owning of slaves, to Canaan being made a slave to his brothers, to the Ten Commandments demonstrating an implicit acceptance of slavery by mentioning it twice, to Jesus not referring to it even though it was widespread in the Roman Empire, to St. Paul telling slaves to obey their masters, and what he writes about the subject in the Epistle to Philemon. They added that slavery removed peoples from non-Christian, pagan cultures to countries where they could hear the Gospel, that just as women were commanded in Scripture to play a subordinate role to men, slaves are also part of a precise social order. They argued that Christians were obliged to obey the civil government and that followers of Jesus should not mix faith with politics — that one is still used today but usually out of convenience when it suits the person repeating it. We may cringe when we read this today but as late as the 1860s these feelings were fairly common among conservative Christians and were all based on a strict reading of Scripture. Jefferson Davis, president of the Confederacy, spoke for many God-fearing people when he said that slavery "was established by decree of Almighty God … it is sanctioned in the Bible, in both Testaments, from Genesis to Revelation … it has existed in all ages, has been found among the people of the highest civilization, and in nations of the highest proficiency in the arts." Alexander Campbell was one of the leading preachers and ministers of the age and one of the senior evangelicals of the time. He wrote that "there is not one verse in the Bible inhibiting slavery, but many regulating it. It is not then, we conclude, immoral." But, we would argue today, they were choosing specific passages of the Bible out of context and in isolation to satisfy their own agendas and rather than applying the love of Christ they were incarcerated by the legalism of those he directly opposed.

So the Bible has to be read and understood intelligently and as the document is supposed to be, and not as a guidebook to be twisted into various shapes to satisfy a pre-existing social and political way of thinking. The term "cafeteria Christian" is often thrown at those of us who believe we have to use the prism of thought, context, and current knowledge to understand Scripture, but if anyone is picking only certain dishes from the theological menu so as to satisfy their own particular appetite it is surely those who feast on the minor elements of the Bible while avoiding the meat and potatoes. Alan Wilson, bishop of Buckingham in the Church of England, made this point rather well when writing in the *Guardian* in October 2014, in response to those of his fellow Christians who argued that the Bible showed quite clearly what marriage was and what it wasn't. It's worth quoting in full.

Generally speaking, Old Testament marriage customs and mores reflect the social mores of the people in the story. Adam and Eve sound like the original simple nuclear family, one plus one for life. In a way, that was all they could be, since they were the only two people in the world at the time.

In Genesis 38, Levirate marriage comes on the scene. This is the involuntary marriage of a man to his brother's widow in order to continue the line. This kind of marriage was still theoretically current enough in Jesus's day for it to be the basis of a question the Sadducees asked him about a bride, seven brothers and resurrection (Matthew 22:23–32).

Deuteronomy institutes another involuntary form of marriage. A virgin automatically becomes the wife of her rapist, who is then required to pay the victim's father 50 shekels for the loss of his property rights. Unlike other Old Testament marriages, these are held to be indissoluble.

In Numbers 31:17–18 we find another form of involuntary marriage. A male soldier is entitled to take as many virgins as he likes for his wives from among his booty, but must kill his other prisoners. In Deuteronomy 21:11–14, marriage is made by selecting a beautiful woman from among the spoils of war, shaving her head and paring her nails. These marriages are dissoluble if she fails to please, but the woman is no longer saleable. Throughout much of the Old Testament, marriage does not require sexual exclusivity. Concubines are allowed, alongside wives. Abraham had only two concubines, where Solomon had 300, along with his 700 wives.

The basic principle of these relationships is that if a woman's father pays a man to take her away, she is his wife. If he pays her father to take her away, she is his concubine.

None of these arrangements, except perhaps that enjoyed by Adam and Eve, would be recognized as marriage today. Pretending that the church's present stance is biblical is not going to fool anyone who doesn't want to be fooled, and fewer and fewer people do.

In other words, be extremely careful in what and how you argue against equal marriage when you try to do so by using the Bible alone because it could backfire dramatically. In Matthew 19 Jesus is asked by a group of Pharisees whether divorce is lawful. He replies that "a man shall leave his father and mother and be joined to his wife, and the two shall become one flesh … So they are no longer two, but one flesh. Therefore what God has joined together, let no one separate." They then ask for clarification of how Moses treated divorce and Jesus replies, "It was because you were so hard-hearted that Moses allowed you to divorce your wives, but from the beginning it was not so. And I say to you, whoever divorces his wife, except for unchastity, and marries another commits adultery."

In Luke 16:18 Jesus says, "Anyone who divorces his wife and marries another commits adultery, and he who marries a woman divorced from her husband commits adultery"; in Matthew 5:32 he says, "But I say to you that anyone who divorces his wife, except on the ground of unchastity, causes her to commit adultery; and whoever marries a divorced woman commits adultery"; in Mark 10:12, "And if she divorces her husband and marries another, she commits adultery"; and the references could continue. In other words, Jesus really does have an awful lot to say about divorce and, boy, is he against it. St. Paul follows suit several times. In his letter to the Romans 7:1–3, he writes: "Do you not know, brethren — for I am speaking to those who know the law — that the law is binding on a person only during that person's lifetime? Thus a married woman is bound by the law to her husband as long as he lives; but if her husband dies, she is discharged from the law concerning the husband. Accordingly, she will be called an adulteress if she lives with another man while her husband is alive. But if her husband dies, she is free from that law, and if she marries another man, she is not an adulteress."

So there we have it. Jesus condemned divorce. Often, loudly, and clearly. He also did so in a culture and an environment that was surprisingly open to divorce and gave women very few rights when marriages did come to an end. Nor was this confined to the Roman and Greek world but was also very much the case within first-century Judaism. Jesus was, as we've already seen, a revolutionary in what he said about any number of things, including divorce. This would have alienated many of his listeners and followers and made him extremely unpopular with those who would have otherwise become followers. But the rebel Christ refused to compromise. Yet most Protestants have allowed divorce for many years, and many denominations have moved with social fashions; they have tended to change with the times. The majority of evangelical churches would say not a word about congregants being divorced, even more than once. Indeed, there are leading clergy and evangelists who are divorced and remarried and their behaviour is considered entirely acceptable. The Roman Catholic Church has a stricter approach to divorce but manages to tackle the problem by its concept of annulment, which is not exactly biblical. Adultery, for example, is not a reason for annulling a marriage, nor, for that matter, is abuse or cruelty. The Catholic Church will annul a marriage if it can be proved that in the eyes of the Church the marriage never actually existed in the first place, was not valid in a Catholic sense, was entered into without full disclosure or a commitment to the demands of the sacrament. Sometimes this is applied with a fair degree of compassion and even lenience, at others times far less so. The inconsistency of decision is a bit of a running joke within Catholic circles. But the point is that Catholicism has found a way to allow divorce, even if they play with the wording.

Jeffrey John is an Anglican priest and dean of St. Albans in Britain. He has written delicately and convincingly about Christian approaches to homosexuality, both as a Christian man who is gay and as someone who was forced by conservative pressure to step away from a bishopric that had been offered to him in 2003. The case was shameful, with an immensely and intensely qualified cleric fulfilling the demands of the Church of England — he is in a celibate, committed relationship with another man — pressurized out of the given position by a loud, sometimes ugly, and often angry coalition of anti-gay Christians both within and outside of his church. His calm, gracious reaction to the campaign was admirable. Let me quote just one brief section:

> The scriptural arguments around gay relationships also run parallel to the scriptural arguments around the ordination of women. Both issues relate to creation ordinances, and especially to particular Pauline passages which seem to rule out both homosexual practice and female leadership on the basis of those ordinances. But of course everything depends on the hermeneutic you apply. A literal exegesis will no doubt rule out same-sex relationships, but it would equally rule out giving any authority to women (let alone ordaining them). Even more strongly, not just on the basis of Paul's teaching, but on the basis of Jesus' own teaching in four separate Gospel passages as well as in Paul, it would rule out the remarriage of divorcees as being equivalent to adultery. I suppose one might just about respect those who reject gay relationships on the basis of scripture, provided they also veil women, forbid them to speak in-church, and condemn the remarried as adulterers.

In some ways the most pertinent of all of the past issues and examples is that of interracial marriage and Christian attitudes toward race in general. Under the apartheid system in South Africa right up until the early 1990s there were Christians and even entire churches that based their defence of racial separation and segregation on Scripture and it wasn't long ago that full denominations in South Africa were proud of such teachings. The vast majority of those churches changed their minds and their understanding of biblical instruction. In the United States, the Virginia trial judge in the 1959 case that led directly to the 1967 U.S. Supreme Court decision that struck down laws in sixteen states that prohibited interracial marriage made the following argument: "Almighty God created the races white, black, yellow, malay and red, and he placed them on separate continents. And but for the interference with his arrangement there would be no cause for such marriages. The fact that he separated the races shows that he did not intend for the races to mix." This was said in living memory — the year I was born, in fact — and such an attitude is far from extinct among certain Christian communities — there are still churches in the southern states of the U.S. that effectively disallow mixed-race couples. As recently as 2011 a major poll found that while 9 percent of Americans opposed interracial marriage, 16 percent of white evangelical Christians were against it; 27 percent of Americans believed mixed marriages were beneficial while only 17 percent of evangelicals thought so. Of course, we have to consider other factors such as class and education but those numbers are too consistent and too obvious to simply disregard. It can't be denied, however, that most Christians today would be appalled at the idea that the Bible stood against people of different races enjoying a lifelong and loving commitment and receiving a church wedding or the sacrament of marriage. They reject those references of the Old Testament that forbid interracial marriages and believe them to apply exclusively to a specific period when the Jewish people were under unique pressures and threats or were given special commands by God that were relevant only thousands of years ago. How odd then, some of the very same people who readily embrace those sophisticated, realistic, compassionate, and sincere arguments about race cannot also apply them to contemporary issues of homosexuality.

So a certain pattern is emerging here and it's not particularly difficult to perceive it. Christians have for generations and even centuries grappled to find ways to reinterpret Scriptural references to divorce, and now try to forget the reality that not so long ago churches resisted demands for basic and self-evident justice by relying on the same Bible that is now used to resist equal marriage. It's not just divorce or racial and gender equality and we could list numerous subjects where a pedantic approach has and will land us in all sorts of trouble. The central problem occurs when we seem to have forgotten the quintessential message of Christ and instead hold onto less vital words to justify prejudice.

I'm not really sure if Jesus openly and explicitly supported same-sex love and equal marriage but I think that there's a good argument to say that he did, and an even better argument to say that he didn't really have an opinion on the subject that applies to the modern world. I am more convinced, however, that he didn't condemn it and that Christians have got this one wrong for far too long.

Let's go back to someone who, according to Luke and Matthew, figures in the rebel Christ's family tree. King David. His relationship with Jonathan is one that has often been explained away as the epitome of brotherly love and male bonding. As David is one of the key characters of Scripture, the Christian or for that matter Jewish world could hardly argue that this was anything other than two noble warriors loving each other as bosom buddies. I remember as a very young boy at the Hebrew classes my Jewish dad urged me to attend on a Sunday morning wondering why we were hearing about two men who sounded like the sort of people we were otherwise told to fear and mock, because the language in the story is certainly challenging. In 1 Samuel 18:1–4 we are told that "when David had finished speaking to Saul, the soul of Jonathan was bound to the soul of David, and Jonathan loved him as his own soul. Saul took him that day and would not let him return to his father's house. Then Jonathan made a covenant with David, because he loved him as his own soul. Jonathan stripped himself of the robe that he was wearing, and gave it to David, and his armor, and even his sword and his bow and his belt." Going back to the Hebrew school reference, I wasn't the only one in the class who giggled when the teacher read this to us in Hebrew as well as English, but this was the 1960s and we were very quickly silenced and told to grow up. But surely it was precisely the grown-up part of us that led to the confusion and the embarrassment. I couldn't help thinking then, and far more so now, what we would conclude if Jonathan were Julie or Gillian — the story would seem much more understandable and "normal." For a man to give what were at that time his most prized possessions, including what he was wearing, to another man the first time they met was baffling to me.

Anybody who knows the story will recall how King Saul, gradually losing his control and probably his mind, turns his temper on David and argues with his son Jonathan over this young man. Jonathan is desperate and concerned and goes to find David in secret to warn him of his father's anger and hysteria. "David rose from beside the stone heap and prostrated himself with his face to the ground. He bowed three times, and they kissed each other, and wept with each other; David wept the more. Then Jonathan said to David, 'Go in peace, since both of us have sworn in the name of the Lord, saying, "The Lord shall be between me and you, and between my descendants and your descendants, forever."' He got up and left and then Jonathan went into the city" (1 Samuel 20:41–42). This was their final encounter, and after Jonathan was killed and David became king he adopted his friend's son as his own, which was extraordinarily rare at the time. And then we have that beautiful, moving but oh so troubling passage in 2 Samuel 1:23, 26–27: "Saul and Jonathan, beloved and lovely! In life and in death they were not divided; they were swifter than eagles, they were stronger than lions.... How the mighty have fallen in the midst of battle! Jonathan lies slain upon your high places. I am distressed for you my brother Jonathan; greatly beloved were you to me; your love to me was wonderful, passing the love of women."

The author of the first and second books of Samuel was close to the royal court and knew the details of David's life, and if we're going to take other biblical passages as literal truth it's difficult to pass this one off as mere poetry and sexually ambivalent hyperbole. Has any genuinely and completely heterosexual man ever told another man that their love was more wonderful than that of a woman? This is more Sparta, Greece, than Sparta, Illinois, a state where there are all sorts of churches where equal marriage is condemned as being sinful. If that's too cryptic, the ancient Spartans accepted and even encouraged their warriors to form homosexual relationships, while in the Midwestern United States, not quite to the same degree.

Some of the Hebrew vocabulary used to describe the relationship between these two men is identical to that used to describe male-female relationships elsewhere in the Old Testament and although there are no explicit references to same-sex romance the story is extremely similar to that of Greek male warriors — see good old Sparta — who were obviously lovers. Remember, the book of Samuel was written centuries before we understood or acknowledged gay relationships in the way we do today. Once again, I'm not claiming that the story of David and Jonathan is without doubt an example of two men who were in fact gay lovers but I am asking people to consider the story and ask honest questions about the example, the language, the attitude of the participants and the writer, and to draw their own conclusions without prejudice. It's what Jesus and his rebel friends would have done.

Fast-forward to the New Testament and the books of both Matthew and Luke. As we've already mentioned more than once, Jesus doesn't refer specifically to homosexuality and certainly doesn't condemn it. But, the argument goes, just because Jesus doesn't actually mention it doesn't mean he didn't think of it as a sin and certainly doesn't imply that he approved of it. True to an extent, but he certainly took the trouble to expose all sorts of sins and to critique religious hypocrisy, but didn't list same-sex attraction as a problem. Nor will it do to argue that homosexuality simply wasn't an issue in the Roman-occupied Jewish world of the time because we know that it most certainly was, and that Jesus's followers and listeners would have been well aware of it. As for Christ not having had to be specific — "after all, he didn't, for example, condemn terrorism or abuse or rape" — this line of reasoning just won't fly. He might not have mentioned terrorism or rape but he did refer to violence and injustice, and that surely covers such crimes.

But back to Matthew and John. One of the most known and loved parts of the story of Jesus, and one that might actually show the contrary to what many Christians argue, concerns a relationship that is deeply moving even at first glance. At second look, however, he may well have been speaking of what he knew to be a loving gay relationship. Matthew 8:5–13 has it thus:

> When he entered Capernaum, a centurion came to him, appealing to him and saying, "Lord, my servant is lying at home paralyzed, in terrible distress." And he said to him, "I will come and cure him." The centurion answered, "Lord, I am not worthy to have you come under my roof; but only speak the word, and my servant will be healed. For I also am a man under authority, with soldiers under me; and I say to one, 'Go,' and he goes, and to another, 'Come,' and he comes, and to my slave, 'Do this,' and the slave does it." When Jesus heard him, he was amazed and said to those who followed him, "Truly I tell you, in no one in Israel have I found such faith. I tell you, many will come from east and west and will eat with Abraham and Isaac and Jacob in the kingdom of heaven, while the heirs of the kingdom will be thrown into the outer darkness, where there will be weeping and gnashing of teeth." And to the centurion Jesus said, "Go; let it be done for you according to your faith." And the servant was healed in that hour.

It's a startling account of a faith so strong that it leads to a miracle, and a faith so deep and fierce from someone who is not Jewish but a Roman soldier, a hated occupier. What we're seeing here is the faith of the gentiles at work, and how Jesus is willing to shower his love and power on all people and not just the Jews. Anybody who trusts so deeply, the story explains, will be rewarded. It's important to realize how hated the Romans were by most of the Jewish people, and in particular by the powerless and the poor, those with whom Jesus spent so much of his time. The Jewish leadership and monarchy had originally turned to the emerging power of Rome as an ally, but by the time of Jesus the Romans were heartily detested. Within a few years a long and violent military uprising would take place, leading to the deaths of many Roman soldiers and even more Jews.

A people without the means to resist will express their contempt in whatever way they can, and one of the regular taunts thrown at the Romans by the Jews was that they participated in homosexual affairs. So it would have been no surprise at all to those listening to this story that the centurion in question had taken this slave as a lover.

Shocking, surprising, and just a modern, liberal ploy to try to justify an acceptance of LGBTQ2 people and equal marriage? Even worse, basing all this on a beloved Jesus story?

Not really. In the Greek original of this Gospel the word used by Matthew to describe the servant of the Roman soldier is *pais*, which in the first century had three different definitions: it could describe a son or could mean "boy"; it could describe a servant; or it could be a specific reference to a servant who was a gay lover, often a younger man or even a teenager. When Luke recounts the same story he uses various Greek words that have other connotations. He describes the centurion's slave as an *entimos doulos*, and while *doulos* was a generic word used to describe a slave it was not used to denote a son or a boy so, in other words, the man in question could not have been the Roman soldier's son. But *entimos* is best translated as "honoured," so we now have someone who was not a son, not an ordinary slave, but someone who, while a servant, was particularly special and loved by the centurion. Interesting.

There are other examples in the Bible of people being healed, but the request for the healing comes from family members or from close, intimate, loved people; in this case it is a hardened soldier, the backbone of the Roman military machine, pleading that his beloved friend — his slave — should be restored to health.

We have to understand the story in context. Yes, there's that word again. Slaves were regarded as property, to be used or abused at will. If they died, so be it. Exceptions might arise if a slave was female and the slave's owner had formed a sexual union with her that became something greater and romantic or if the slave was male and after many years of service had become an adviser or an intellectual companion to an owner or a father figure to the children of the family. None of those examples explain this incident and if we combine these circumstances with the popular understanding of Roman soldiers and their sexual use of both male and female slaves a certain picture emerges that certainly causes us to rethink what we are reading.

Beyond the Gospels, the Acts of the Apostles also offers an anecdote that merits deeper discussion. In chapter 8:26–40 we're told that an angel says to Philip,

> "Get up and go toward the south to the road that goes down from Jerusalem to Gaza." (This is a wilderness road.) So he got up and went. Now there was an Ethiopian eunuch, a court official of the Candace, queen of the Ethiopians, in charge of her entire treasury. He had come to Jerusalem to worship and was returning home; seated in his chariot, he was reading the prophet Isaiah. Then the Spirit said to Philip, "Go over to this chariot and join it." So Philip ran up to it and heard him reading the prophet Isaiah. He asked, "Do you understand what you are reading?" He replied, "How can I, unless someone guides me?" And he invited Philip to get in and sit beside him. Now the passage of the scripture that he was reading was this:

> *"Like a sheep he was led to the slaughter,*
> *and like a lamb silent before its shearer,*
> *so he does not open his mouth.*
> *In his humiliation justice was denied him.*
> *Who can describe his generation?*
> *For his life is taken away from the earth."*

> The eunuch asked Philip, "About whom, may I ask you, does the prophet say this, about himself or about someone else?" Then Philip began to speak, and starting with this scripture, he proclaimed to him the good news about Jesus. As they were going along the road, they came to some water; and the eunuch said, "Look, here is water! What is to prevent me from being baptized?" He commanded the chariot to stop, and both of them, Philip and the eunuch, went down into the water, and Philip baptized him. When they came up out of the water, the Spirit of the Lord snatched Philip away; the eunuch saw him no more, and went on his way rejoicing. But Philip found himself at Azotus, and as he was passing through the region, he proclaimed the good news to all the towns until he came to Caesarea.

The Greek word used in Acts of the Apostles is *eunouchos* or "guardian" or "keeper" of the couch and was used only when describing men who were completely trusted by monarchs, royal families, and rulers. The *eunouchos* would be employed to care for and guard women, often high-ranking women, in similarly high-ranking families, and as such had to be beyond risk. They often became powerful and important themselves and in this case the eunuch in question was treasurer to the queen of Ethiopia. As the word indicates, some of these men were literally castrated, but we now know with our modern understanding of science and physiology that castration does not necessarily expunge all sexual desire and can even make men more sexually and physically aggressive. Those who lived two thousand years ago may not have understood the intricacies of where and how testosterone is made in the male body, but they would have surely known by tradition and experience that physical castration was not always effective. It prevented procreation but not necessarily the desire to have sex. This is where the concept of what were known as "natural" or "born" eunuchs comes into play. There are numerous references in ancient culture to men who had no sexual or romantic attraction to women and were thus classified as eunuchs even though they were physically intact. We obviously have no idea whether the man mentioned in Acts was a physical eunuch or not but we do know that he would have been associated with a group of men who were regarded as having links to homosexuality. As far back as Deuteronomy 23:1 the Bible stated that "no one whose testicles are crushed or whose penis is cut off shall be admitted to the assembly of the Lord," and by the time of Jesus and the early church this sorry and unfortunate category included even those who could not have children; indeed, first-century Judaism refused conversion to such men. But here we have Philip refusing to judge or condemn this man and instead inviting him into the church and into a relationship with Jesus Christ. He didn't ask the eunuch to change his nature if he was gay, he didn't read him passages from an ancient text, and didn't inquire whether he was a literal eunuch, or someone defined as such because he was homosexual, but merely loved him unconditionally.

It's this overwhelming quality of unconditional love that so characterizes the ministry of Jesus, yet he combines it with an unprecedented understanding of human nature. As described earlier, Christ is radical in his criticisms of divorce partly because of the sheer injustice involved, and the pain, poverty, and disgrace it caused to women. This led to some of his male followers questioning the strictness of the teaching, and to something that applies to this chapter. If divorce is so wrong, some listeners responded, maybe it would be better not to marry at all. Jesus responds in Matthew 19:11–12, "Not everyone can accept this teaching, but only those to whom it is given. For there are eunuchs who have been so from birth, and there are eunuchs who have been made eunuchs by others, and there are eunuchs who have made themselves eunuchs for the sake of the kingdom of heaven. Let anyone accept this who can."

So here we have Jesus listing three types of men who should not marry: those who have been made eunuchs by others, and, we must assume, have been physically castrated; those who have opted to be eunuchs and, we assume, have chosen celibacy so as to devote their lives entirely to the service of God; and a third group consisting of men who were born eunuchs. If the latter is meant to be men who were born without testicles we are entering the realm of absurdity — such events are so incredibly rare to be irrelevant and would never have been included in such a statement about the nature of marriage, faith, and God. More than this, other such references in ancient texts to those born as eunuchs never refer to boys born with deformities but to something entirely different. So is Jesus speaking in entirely neutral and non-judgmental terms of men who were born gay? Many modern theologians believe exactly this.

So far these references have been to men and to male homosexuality, but consider the story of Naomi in the Hebrew Scriptures. She and her husband Elimelech are from Bethlehem — literally "City of Bread," one of the most significant towns in the Bible, and to be so literally and metaphorically important in the life of Jesus. In Naomi's case a major famine forces her and her family to flee to Moab, which is part of another nation, and a different culture. Here Naomi's husband dies, and many years later her sons marry two women named Ruth and Orpah. But tragedy strikes again and both sons die, leaving the three women alone and isolated. That isolation meant something entirely different in the society of the time, where women were generally either daughters or wives. They were natural victims to the men and circumstances around them if they didn't have any male support. There are various precedents in biblical texts such as First and Second Kings and Genesis 38 where we see how vulnerable widows in particular were, and it's no surprise that Naomi decides to return to Bethlehem even though the city is still troubled. She tells her daughters-in-law to also return to their own homes. Orpah does so but Ruth cannot. She explains that she is too close to Naomi to leave her and we are told that she "clung" to Naomi. The word in Hebrew used to describe how she felt and how she acted is *dabaq*, which is the same word used in Genesis to describe Adam's attachment to Eve. Ruth says, "Do not press me to leave you or to turn back from following you! Where you go, I will go; where you lodge I will lodge; your people shall be my people, and your God my God. Where you die, I will die — there will I be buried. May the Lord do thus and so to me, and more as well, if even death parts me from you!"

These are sentiments still often used even today when speaking of or conducting a marriage. If we combine these with the meaning of that word *dabaq*, we have a little explaining to do. When the word is used in the context of Adam and Eve it refers to a man leaving his parents, growing up, and "clinging" to his wife. That can't simply be dismissed as coincidence — language is specific and used with a purpose. Scripture then tells us of Ruth and Naomi's life together and how they were devoted, and how they sacrificed for one another. Ruth does marry in the end but to a man much older than her and in a union based not on love but on the need to find someone to help Ruth and Naomi survive financially. Eventually Ruth has a baby boy from her marriage of convenience, but it's significant how the father, Boaz, is not mentioned in the announcement of the birth. We are, on the other hand, told of Naomi's delight at the news. The local women state that "a son has been born to Naomi" (Ruth 4:17) and tell her that Ruth, "who loves you, is more to you than seven sons" (Ruth 4:15).

Again, just as I said earlier, I'm not absolutely convinced that this story is about a same-sex couple and I would never demand for a moment that Christians have to understand it as such. It's foremost about devotion and love; it could be about mixed-race romance; it could be about the nature of conversion and the definition of who and what is a follower of God, or who is Jewish; it could be about tolerance and the non-racial nature of God's plan. But it could also be about something else entirely. Ambiguity can play havoc with those who think that they have all of the answers.

Which brings us to those texts that are supposed to close the argument once and for all. These are apparently the difficult bits, the challenging quotes, or what have been labelled the "clobber" passages of Scripture. There are very few of them and most require a new and informed interpretation. The British evangelical leader Steve Chalke describes these half-dozen verses as "the six bullets in the gun." Alas, he's right, and they have been used as ammunition far too often, and with dark and painful results. Because some people who use them shoot to kill. Chalke, by the way, is one of the victims of the firing squad. He's a highly respected Christian leader who became a popular and accepted spokesman for the Christian world through his work on television. There were few more effective Christian voices in the entire country. He remains an orthodox Christian but in 2014 made public his change of heart over equal marriage and LGBTQ2 rights. As a straight man and a follower of Christ, he announced, he had after much prayer and reflection changed his position. He was immediately condemned by many of his fellow evangelicals and expelled from various Christian bodies and groups.

Let's start with the movies. In 1962 Pathé, SGC, and Titanus co-produced a movie called *Sodom and Gomorrah*, known in the United States as *The Last Days of Sodom and Gomorrah.* Bible epics were popular at the time, and with the dashing Stewart Granger, a sexy co-star, and an impressive cast, great things were expected. As it turned out it was a truly awful movie and the line that perhaps best sums up the ineptitude and unintentional humour of the thing came very early with the cry, "Watch out for Sodomite patrols!" Watch out, indeed. The movie came and went but Sodom is still discussed and quoted to a degree that is breathtaking when we consider its meagre historical and theological importance. Sodom has a great deal for which to answer. Silly movies aside, the hurt and damage caused by a callow and rash interpretation of this relatively trivial and often totally misunderstood slice of Old Testament story is virtually beyond measure. I often think that heaven must weep at the brokenness, devastation, suicide, family breakdown, and sheer terror provoked and produced by a few words written so long ago, and at how eager so many of Christ's followers are to use this story not to better appreciate God but to better exclude some of his loved and cherished creatures.

The centre of the story is contained in Genesis 19:4–6: "Before they lay down, the men of the city, the men of Sodom, both young and old, all the people to the last man, surrounded the house; and they called to Lot, 'Where are the men who came to you tonight? Bring them out to us, so that we may know them.' Lot went out of the door to the men, shut the door after him." Good old Lot. But let's take a closer look at what was actually going on here.

Abraham, formerly known as Abram, one of the central figures not only of the Christian but also the Jewish and Muslim faiths, has a nephew called Lot who went to live in Sodom, which was then regarded as one of the more modern and advanced cities of the ancient Middle East, but also considered a place of great evil. For Lot it was an alternative to the rural desert life of his uncle who lived an essentially nomadic existence. But along with all that modernity, wealth, and comfort went wickedness; the city of Sodom was decadent and populated by immoral people, although we're not told exactly what sort of evil they got up to, but are given some broad brush strokes of the nasty picture. Abraham is blessed by God and meets with three angels close to the Oaks of Mamre. Lot, however, doesn't do as well and is captured as a prisoner, then rescued by Abraham, and eventually settles in Sodom. But God tells Abraham that because of its reputation for evil, Sodom is to be destroyed as an example to warn others. Two of the three angels from Mamre are sent to Sodom to find out if the stories of evil are true and, of course, they visit Abraham's nephew to stay, to be fed, and to be looked after, and so on. Lot doesn't realize his visitors are angels but he knows that strangers must be protected and treated kindly, both because this is the holy and righteous way to live and also because he himself had been in such a position not so long ago. All proceeds well but in the evening the people from the city come to Lot's door, having learned that he has welcomed two strangers, and they demand that Lot send his guests out to them so that they might "know them" — the Hebrew word used in Genesis is sometimes, though not always, used to denote sex or sexual intercourse, and while some scholars doubt that meaning in this context we can probably accept it in this case as meaning sex. Lot is outraged and argues with those outside his door, explaining that what they want is wrong and evil. As an alternative he suggests that he send his virgin daughters out to them instead, but the people outside the door insist on those apparently irresistible strangers and try to smash their way inside the house. As a consequence, the angels cause those shouting and threatening to become blind, and then explain to Lot that he and his family have to leave Sodom because God will indeed destroy the place. The following day a great fire is sent from heaven and Sodom is wiped out and its population killed.

The story isn't new to most of us and for centuries it's been the foundational episode for the Christian assumption that homosexuality is evil and immoral, and in consequence has led to the marginalization, condemnation, and even persecution and slaughter of LGBTQ2 people.

But it doesn't require a theologian or an ancient historian to realize that there are some gigantic inconsistencies about the story and some worrying implications. First of all, it's not in any way certain that this text was always considered to apply to homosexuality and may well have been given that connotation for the first time by Jewish scribes living between the era of the Old and New Testaments, who were anxious to further differentiate Jews from gentiles. Knowing that several non-Jewish cultures of the time accepted homosexuality, they attempted to define homosexuality as one of the key characteristics of gentile immorality and insisted that it had been condemned by God in Genesis to the point of the total destruction of a city and a people. So, understanding the chronology of all this matters very much indeed if we are to respect the Bible in the way it deserves.

Beyond how the very meaning may have been changed centuries after the text was written, today the terms *sodomy* and *sodomites*, while archaic and offensive to most people, are still used. They were once commonplace. The words in the story are vitally important and we have to get them right if we're to appreciate the meaning and purpose of all this. The Bible says that "the men of Sodom, both young and old, all the people to the last man" come to Lot's house, to his door, and shout that his guests must be brought to them. Not just some of the people in the city, not just those who were known to be homosexual, not just the adults, but all of them. Even the most committed conspiracy theorist or paranoid homophobe would have a problem with those sorts of numbers! Quite clearly this is absurd. Also, remember that Lot offers his virgin daughters to the hysterical mob in place of the two male strangers, which would indicate that the would-be rapists outside the door desire not men as such but any person they can gang-rape and abuse. Not exactly the model of family values.

This is surely an account not of homosexuality but of the evils of animalistic sex, rape, abuse, the treatment of other people as sexual objects. In ancient cultures and even in the modern world, rape of captured men, and, of course, women, by conquering soldiers is an expression less of lust and sexuality than of dominance and sadism. Rape was and is still a weapon. In Judges 19 there is another and lesser known reference to gang rape where a mob surround a man's house:

> The men of the city, a perverse lot, surrounded the house, and started pounding on the door. They said to the old man,

> the master of the house, "Bring out the man who came into your house, so that we may have intercourse with him." And the man, the master of the house, went out to them and said to them, "No, my brothers, do not act so wickedly. Since this man is my guest, do not do this vile thing. Here are my virgin daughter and his concubine; let me bring them out now. Ravish them and do whatever you want to them; but against this man do not do such a vile thing." But the men would not listen to him. So the man seized his concubine, and put her out to them. They wantonly raped her, and abused her all through the night until the morning. And as the dawn began to break, they let her go.

Frankly, it's a little difficult to draw too many conclusions from all this and quite dangerous to even try to do so without a great deal of qualification and questioning. Yet the story of Sodom is used times beyond counting to explain not ancient crimes and punishment but to justify modern discrimination and even assault and murder.

There are also references in the Bible itself to the story of Sodom that contradict the standard understanding that it's about homosexuality. There are around twenty mentions of Sodom in Scripture and not one of them speaks of homosexuals. In Ezekiel, for example, we are told, "This was the guilt of your sister Sodom: she and her daughters had pride, excess of food, and prosperous ease, but did not aid the poor and needy. They were haughty, and did abominable things before me; therefore I removed them when I saw it." So rather than condemning homosexuality, the book of Ezekiel is using the Sodom story to expose the sins of pride, gluttony, complacency, and sloth; indifference to the poor; arrogance; and excess wealth. Isaiah speaks of Sodom as an example of lack of and abuse of justice, Jeremiah speaks of it in terms of general immorality, in Wisdom we are reminded that the men of Sodom refused to accept the strangers who visited their city, and Ecclesiasticus 16 says that the sin of Sodom was not homosexuality but pride. In the New Testament Jesus speaks about those cities that refuse to greet and welcome his disciples and warns that their fate will be worse than that of Sodom. Not, remember, because of any sexual crime that has been committed there but because they have shown a lack of hospitality and have refused to embrace visitors.

The Sodom myth took on its more modern resonance as late as the eleventh century when Peter Damian — a cardinal who was later made a Doctor of the Church — wrote *The Book of Gomorrah* for Pope Leo IX:

> Truly, this vice is never to be compared with any other vice because it surpasses the enormity of all vices.... It defiles everything, stains everything, pollutes everything. And as for itself, it permits nothing pure, nothing clean, nothing other than filth....
>
> The miserable flesh burns with the heat of lust; the cold mind trembles with the rancor of suspicion; and in the heart of the miserable man chaos boils like Tartarus [Hell] ... In fact, after this most poisonous serpent once sinks its fangs into the unhappy soul, sense is snatched away, memory is borne off, the sharpness of the mind is obscured. It becomes unmindful of God and even forgetful of itself. This plague undermines the foundation of faith, weakens the strength of hope, destroys the bond of charity; it takes away justice, subverts fortitude, banishes temperance, blunts the keenness of prudence.
>
> And what more should I say since it expels the whole host of the virtues from the chamber of the human heart and introduces every barbarous vice as if the bolts of the doors were pulled out.

And with that the accusation of sodomy and the persecution of those labelled as sodomites began its dark, bloody stain that continues to this day. James Kugel, who has served as both Starr Professor Emeritus of Classical and Modern Hebrew Literature at Harvard and chair of the Institute for the History of the Jewish Bible at Bar-Ilan University in Tel Aviv, has written that early interpreters were "perplexed about the city of Sodom. God destroyed it because of the terrible things that were being done there — but what exactly were those things? Strangely, the Genesis narrative does not say." Richard Elliott Friedman, professor of Hebrew and Comparative Literature at the University of California, San Diego, doesn't even believe that we have the gender of the crowd correct. He believes that there is "no basis for this whatever. The text says that two people come to Sodom, and that all of the people of Sodom come and say, 'Let's know them.' The homosexuality interpretation apparently comes from misunderstanding the Hebrew word 'anasim' to mean 'men,' instead of people."

Would that it ended there. Those Christians who oppose the demands of the LGBTQ2 community argue that if Genesis is a little ambiguous and Sodom not sufficiently convincing we have what it says in Leviticus. But what does it actually say in the third book of the Bible? There are in fact two references in Leviticus to homosexuality: 18:22 has "You shall not lie with a male as with a woman; it is an abomination." But the same passage also commands, "You shall not approach a woman to uncover her nakedness while she is in her menstrual uncleanness. You shall not have sexual relations with your kinsman's wife, and defile yourself with her. You shall not give any of your offspring to sacrifice them to Molech, and so profane the name of your God: I am the Lord.... You shall not have sexual relations with any animal and defile yourself with it, nor shall any woman give herself to an animal to have sexual relations with it: it is perversion."

Not sure how relevant this is to the modern age, and if some of it appears grimly archaic and obviously applicable only to the ancient culture in question, why would not all of it appear grimly archaic and applicable only to the ancient culture in question?

Some historical background first. The writing of Leviticus probably dates back to the Jewish exile in Babylon and was written to encourage childbirth and an increased Jewish population during a time of enormous pressure on the Jews to convert, intermarry, and assimilate. There was a genuine danger of the Jewish people disappearing in their diaspora, and if they ever were to resettle in Israel they had to have the numbers to do so. This particular part of Leviticus was likely written by someone we know of as "The Priestly Writer" and was probably the same person who gave us in Genesis the creation story and the command to "go forth and multiply." Its commands were also a way to distinguish Jewish from Babylonian culture and society at a time when Babylon seemed increasingly tempting and welcoming to the Jews — enormous numbers of exiled Jewish people gradually came not only to accept but to embrace those who had conquered them. Ancient Babylon was not only tolerant of homosexuality but may well have included it in local forms of worship, and while Jews were not expected to participate they would be required to accept.

The prohibition around homosexuality is also deeply woven into ancient attitudes toward gender, women, and masculinity. We are speaking here of a culture of several thousand years ago where there was a steel-like patriarchy and, in a literal sense, patriarchs; indeed, the original patriarchs. This was a male-dominated society where masculine characteristics were the model and the rule. The Leviticus reference is not to same-sex partnerships as we know and understand them today, and such an interpretation of the text would be horribly reductive.

As we've already established, Jesus never even mentions the subject. I know this might sound repetitive but it's still generally assumed that Christ pronounced on this issue and as we have seen he simply doesn't, unless it is implicitly through his acceptance of a centurion's love for a male slave. Paul, however, does do so, or at least appears to do so. In his Letter to the Romans, 1:24–27:

> Therefore God gave them up in the lusts of their hearts to impurity, to the degrading of their bodies among themselves, because they exchanged the truth about God for a lie and worshiped and served the creature rather than the Creator, who is blessed forever! Amen.
>
> For this reason God gave them up to degrading passions. Their women exchanged natural intercourse for unnatural, and in the same way also the men, giving up natural intercourse with women, were consumed with passion for one another. Men committed shameless acts with men and received in their own persons the due penalty for their error.

To understand this properly, however, we need to show what Paul wrote both directly before and directly after this oft-quoted paragraph. Leading up to this Paul writes in 21–23,

> For though they knew God, they did not honor him as God or give thanks to him, but they became futile in their thinking, and their senseless minds were darkened. Claiming to be wise, they became fools; and they exchanged the glory of the immortal God for images resembling a mortal human being or birds or four-footed animals or reptiles.

And immediately afterward:

> And since they did not see fit to acknowledge God, God gave them up to a debased mind and to things that should not be done. They were filled with every kind of wickedness, evil, covetousness, malice. Full of envy, murder, strife, deceit, craftiness, they are gossips, slanderers, God-haters, insolent, haughty, boastful, inventors of evil, rebellious toward parents, foolish, faithless, heartless, ruthless. They know God's decree, that those who practice such things deserve

> to die – yet they not only do them but even applaud others who practice them.

So if we follow the order of all this and not just isolate the verses ostensibly about homosexuality, we see a strict chronology develop. Paul writes first about those who refuse to acknowledge and honour God, then about how those people begin to worship idols, next how they become far more interested in earthly than spiritual pursuits, then how they abandon their natural desires for sex with people of the same gender, and finally how they disrespect their parents and are proud, envious, malicious, and argumentative. What he is writing about, in fact, is how they come to reject and hate God. This letter is written to a church composed both of Jewish believers in Christ and gentiles who have abandoned various pagan religions and cults for Christianity. In the first part of the letter Paul seems to be criticizing those gentiles who haven't lived up to the faith, and in the second he addresses the failing of the Jewish believers.

But what is it primarily about? Paul is obviously angry and disappointed at those who have exchanged what is right for what is wrong; he packages various failings, errors, and sins together, all of them resulting in a falling away from the glory of the one, true God. He uses the words *nature* and *natural* and is specific in his choice of language. Yet in 1 Corinthians Paul asks us, "Does not nature itself teach you that if a man wears long hair, it is degrading to him?" In other words, we have to understand what is being written in terms of contemporary attitudes. Paul's question about hair length would have seemed bizarre even a few years later, let alone several centuries later. Beware of taste masquerading as morality. For example, military swagger amongst many of Napoleon's cavalry troopers was indicated by long, flowing hair; the same martial spirit a century later in the French army was shown by close, cropped haircuts.

Paul is also speaking here of idolatry and of putting selfish desires and lusts before the worship of God. It's about forgetting God and expunging him from the human equation, and Paul writes that this failing is demonstrated by all sorts of behaviour, including straight men indulging in what is unnatural to their characters. To gay men and women following Christ today, who have no inclination to worship anything or any person other than God and who have only ever felt romance and attraction to those of the same gender, this condemnation simply doesn't apply, and has no spiritual or ethical meaning at all. It should matter not a jot to the homosexual, but my goodness it matters a great deal to the homophobe.

There was no appreciation at this time that homosexuality wasn't mere choice made by otherwise heterosexual men, but something innate. Yet the notion of "exchanging" is precisely what Paul refers to in his Letter to the Romans. Neither he nor his contemporaries were writing of gay couples but of sexual exploitation, of pagan abuse, and of physical aggression and loveless sex. Professor John Boswell wrote,

> The persons Paul condemns are manifestly not homosexual: what he derogates are homosexual acts committed by apparently heterosexual persons....
>
> It is not clear that Paul distinguished in his thoughts or writings between gay persons (in the sense of permanent sexual preference) and heterosexuals who simply engaged in periodic homosexual behavior. It is in fact unlikely that many Jews of his day recognized such a distinction, but it is quite apparent that – whether or not he was aware of their existence – Paul did not discuss gay persons but only homosexual acts committed by heterosexual persons.

James Brownson's book *Bible, Gender, Sexuality: Reframing the Church's Debate on Same-Sex Relationships* is a remarkable work on many levels, but what he says about Paul's Letter to the Romans is especially revealing. He speaks of how Paul is not being generic in his words but is directly referring to the Roman emperors Gaius and the infamous Caligula and their international reputations for immorality and indulgence. Paul's readers and listeners would have known exactly whom he was describing and condemning, and it may well be that it is the lifestyles of the Roman, pagan leaders rather than same-sex attraction. He writes:

> First of all, Gaius is closely linked to the practice of idolatry. The Roman writer Suetonius reports how Gaius "set up a special temple to his own godhead, with priests and with victims of the choicest kind." Another Roman writer, Dio Cassius, comments negatively on how Gaius was the only emperor to claim to be divine and to be the recipient of worship during his own lifetime. Gaius also tried at one point to erect a statue of himself in the Temple in Jerusalem; he was dissuaded only by a delegation from Herod Agrippa. Hence the link between Gaius and idolatry would have been well-known indeed, particularly in Jewish circles. But Gaius also serves as "Exhibit A" for out-of-control lust. Suetonius reports how Gaius "lived in perpetual incest with all his sisters, and at a large banquet he placed each of them in turn below him, while his wife reclined above." He records gruesome examples of Gaius's arbitrary violence, vindictiveness, and cruelty. Later, Suetonius chronicles Gaius's sexual liaisons with the wives of dinner guests, raping them in an adjoining room and then returning to the banquet to comment on their performance. Various same-sex sexual encounters between Gaius and other men are similarly recounted. Finally, a military officer whom he had sexually humiliated joined a conspiracy to murder him, which they did less than four years into his reign. Suetonius records that Gaius was stabbed through the genitals when he was murdered. One wonders whether we can hear an echo of this gruesome story in Paul's comments in Romans 1:27: "Men

> committed shameless acts with men and received in their own person the due penalty for their error." Gaius Caligula graphically illustrates the reality of which Paul speaks in Romans 1: the movement from idolatry to insatiable lust to every form of depravity, and the violent murderous reprisal that such behavior engenders.

On a cursory reading, there are clearly passages in Paul's Letter to the Romans that are uncomfortable for liberal-minded Christians. But we can do better than that. Former archbishop of Canterbury Rowan Williams, one of the finest living theologians, made this point back in 2007 when he spoke at the University of Toronto. He told his audience that the passage in Romans that appears to refer to homosexuality was, if anything, a warning to Christians that they should not be self-righteous, and that its primary point was most certainly not about homosexuality at all. He argued that Paul was telling the church that whenever they condemned others they are condemning themselves and he believed that the letter doesn't favour any side of the Christian argument in the debate. Other historians and theologians have argued that Romans is about all forms of non-procreative sex; that it's about pedophilia, polygamy, or incest, or the use of slaves for dominant, sadistic sex.

So to the last of the "clobber" verses, both again from Paul — 1 Corinthians 6:7–11:

> In fact, to have lawsuits at all with one another is already a defeat for you. Why not rather be wronged? Why not rather be defrauded? But you yourselves wrong and defraud – and believers at that.
>
> Do you not know that wrongdoers will not inherit the kingdom of God? Do not be deceived! Fornicators, idolaters, adulterers, male prostitutes, sodomites, thieves, the greedy, drunkards, revilers, robbers – none of these will inherit the kingdom of God. And this is what some of you used to be. But

> you were washed, you were sanctified, you were justified in the name of the Lord Jesus Christ and in the Spirit of our God.

And 1 Timothy 1:8–11:

> Now we know that the law is good, if one uses it legitimately. This means understanding that the law is laid down not for the innocent but for the lawless and disobedient, for the godless and sinful, for the unholy and profane, for those who kill their father or mother, for murderers, fornicators, sodomites, slave traders, liars, perjurers, and whatever else is contrary to the sound teaching that conforms to the glorious gospel of the blessed God, which he entrusted to me.

There are two Greek terms used by Paul that should be clarified: *malakoi* and *arsenokoites*. The first means "softies" and it's used elsewhere in Scripture and in general Greek to refer to clothes as well as to men; this is especially significant as there are other Greek words that could have been used that apply only to men who are the passive partners in homosexual sex. *Malakoi*, on the other hand, is used to describe all sorts of soft or even pleasant activities such as fine food, warm baths, or clothes that are comfortable rather than rough on the skin. Some gay men may be soft, but that's nothing more than a caricature. The homosexual troops of the Hellenic armies, for example, were renowned for their courage and toughness. They were hardly thought of as softies by their enemies. *Arsenokoites* is an equally bewildering choice as it's a contrived word, one that was conceived by Paul and had no earlier reference in biblical or non-biblical Greek. Its literal translation is "male-bedder," or a man who is willing to take the place of a woman in bed or become the passive partner in gay sex. But there's also a deeper meaning because the word is listed along with those who exploit people financially or take economic advantage of others.

In that case, we're probably better off thinking of male-bedders as male prostitutes or rent boys, younger men selling themselves to older men — often heterosexual men — for money and gain. Subsequently, it's used in post-biblical ancient literature to describe an economic sin or a crime. Both Clement of Alexandria and John Chrysostom discuss homosexuality in their writings but neither used the word *arsenokoitai* other than when they are quoting the very lists Paul uses in Corinthians. If we're to construe anything from this it's that Paul was not speaking of homosexuality as such but about those who used sexuality, of whatever kind, for financial benefit. We have to ask why such a literate man, so well versed in various languages and so in control of his vocabulary and meaning, would invent a new word that wouldn't be familiar to his readers, rather than use words for "homosexual" that were far better known.

Then there is the list of activities Paul provides that will apparently close the door to the kingdom of God. They include slander, perjury, drunkenness, greed, and lying. None of them are to be admired but none receive anything like the criticism given by conservative Christians to the LGBTQ2 community. There are more than a few critics of gay people who have been a little greedy, have drunk too much, and even told the odd lie. None of them, surely, would agree that any of these would shut the doors of paradise.

The more we learn about the nature of the first century and about the language, religion, and culture of the time the more we question long-held opinions about what the Bible actually teaches on this issue. If I had any hair left I would wear it as I liked and know God loved me. I will mix the cloths of my clothes and know that God loves me. I eat pork and bacon and even mix milk and meat and know that God loves me. But, in all honesty, I seldom eat shellfish — not that it would stop God loving me, but I just don't like shellfish very much. I'm also straight. Not because being gay would stop God loving me and loving my partner, and blessing our marriage, but because I'm simply not gay. If I were gay, though, it would make being a Christian so much more difficult; and God wouldn't love that at all.

Dr. Daniel A. Helminiak is the author of the seminal work *What the Bible Really Says About Homosexuality*. He writes,

> The literal approach to the Bible claims not to interpret the Bible but merely to take it for what it obviously says. The words of the Bible in modern translation are taken to mean what they mean to the reader today. On this basis the Bible is said to condemn homosexuality in a number of places. But a historical-critical approach reads the Bible in its original historical and cultural context. This approach takes the Bible to mean, as best as can be determined, what its human authors intended to say in their own time and in their own way. Understood on its own terms, the Bible was not addressing our current questions about sexual ethics. The Bible does not condemn gay sex as we understand it today. The fact of the matter is simple enough. The Bible never addresses that question. More than that, the Bible seems deliberately unconcerned about it.

Professor Helminiak happens to be an ordained Roman Catholic priest. So, things are not always what they seem. That's something the rebel Christ reminds us of repeatedly.

A personal story. Bobby is from Kampala, Uganda, and is twenty-seven years old. She comes from a middle-class Anglican Christian family, though her mother converted from Islam when she married Bobby's father. Bobby has two brothers and one sister, and gained a degree in economics from a university in the British midlands — she insisted I not provide precise details because she is frightened of the possible consequences for her family, and because she promised her father that she would not, to use his words, "embarrass and disgrace" the family. She returned to Uganda after university but left again in

2014, and has no plans to return unless the politics of the country and the Ugandan church's attitudes toward homosexuality change radically, and gay people are given acceptance and protection.

> I grew up with a certain privilege, and compared to most people in Uganda we were wealthy and secure. It was rather idyllic really in that we had a nanny and a gardener, the climate was gorgeous, my parents were loving and considerate and I went to a private school that was very English. I always thought myself as a bit of a tomboy – do people still use that phrase? – and I suppose people around me thought the same thing. It was all a bit of a cliché really. I played sport with the boys, climbed trees, didn't like wearing dresses and so on. There was never anything sexual or romantic in my life and I don't remember even really knowing what lesbianism was. I'd heard about homosexuality from one of the ministers in church and from an American who came to our particular church to speak about it, and what a threat it was and how much damage it had done in the United States. But I thought for some reason that only men could be gay; it wasn't until university that I found out that homosexual didn't mean love between men but love for someone like yourself. We never discussed these things at home but when we went to church, and we were a very Anglican family, the subject seemed to come up again and again. On the one hand we were told that it was a foreign problem and that Ugandans weren't really gay, and on the other hand we were warned that gays were everywhere and a threat to everything we cared about. I always remember my little brother saying to my father, "Daddy, monsters aren't real are they? But homosexuals are real aren't they?" It was like that: monsters, gays, terrorists, all the same I suppose.
>
> It was only when my friends began to start dating that I thought something might be different about me. I just didn't

want to go out with boys. Not with girls either though – I just wasn't interested in dating. I was about fifteen then and this went on for about two years. Then one night at a party we all got a bit drunk, and that was easy for me because my family were pretty strict and I'd hardly any experience of alcohol at all. I was waiting to go to the bathroom and started talking to another girl who was in the line and then we were the only two there. Suddenly she kissed me. Nothing aggressive or even passionate. Just a little kiss. She apologized quickly, said she had got the wrong idea and pleaded with me not to say anything. She must have thought I was offended or frightened and that I would tell someone. I can't quite remember what I said but I know I walked away, went home and felt so good about it, so good about myself, so calm, so complete really. It felt as though this was what life and happiness were supposed to feel like, and that it was all supposed to have happened.

I asked around my friends about this girl and found out who she was. Weeks later – because I was naive and a bit scared and totally inexperienced – I waited by her home and then spoke to her. From then on we were, well, best friends I suppose. I don't think we ever did anything more than hugged and held hands. The occasional kiss maybe but it was so innocent. That was all. All without any guilt, all so lovely, so charming. I didn't think of myself as gay or a lesbian or homosexual or anything. All I knew was that I was happy and that was all. Then I wasn't happy. She was hit by a car and killed, and the driver didn't even stop. It could have been an accident and I know I might sound paranoid but I am convinced that she was killed because of who and what she was. She came from a poorer background than mine was and a few girls, and more boys, who were gay from her sort of background had been beaten, raped, or murdered at around that time. I was sure then and I am sure now that my first love, this good and sweet and entirely blameless young woman, was killed like an animal because she was gay. You might think it's the grief speaking but you don't know Africa and you don't know Uganda.

I went to see the priest at our church because he had known our family for a long time and I trusted him. What a fool I was. He blamed her for what had happened and said I had been led astray, and even though he had promised not to do so he went to tell my parents. They were angry but not violent. They said I was imagining she was murdered in just the same way that I was imagining that I was a lesbian. It sounds ridiculous as I retell all this but my punishment was to be sent away and in my case to be sent to a university in Britain so I could be free of what was influencing me in Uganda. Most Ugandan gays can't even afford to leave the town and I was being paid to leave the country and have a great time at a university! In Britain of course I came out as gay completely and almost immediately and have had various relationships. I went back home afterwards and told my family about who I was, and they said I was no longer welcome at home but that they would continue to support me financially. They were heartbroken. I know I should be angry with them but I can't be and I still love them. It's so hard for them because they have been told for so many years by priests and ministers and missionaries that homosexuality is evil and wrong. I blame the church and I blame American Christians a great deal too. I saw the influence and the money that came from the United States around all of this. I'm not saying that native Ugandan Christians aren't guilty because they are, and homophobia is part of our country's religious history but the church in the west should be trying to help us and not making things worse. Do I still miss her? Every single day.

Bobby found a church in Britain that accepts and affirms her, and remains a faithful Christian. She certainly knows about crucifixion. So much suffering, caused by so much hatred, based on so much misunderstanding. Jesus wept.

Chapter 4

Life Begins at ... Being Really, Really Angry About Abortion

In 2020, a United Methodist pastor in Birmingham, Alabama, named Dave Barnhart wrote something on social media about critics of abortion that provoked quite a reaction from all sides of the debate. He said that the "unborn" are a very convenient group to apparently be active about because they don't make any demands of you and they're not morally complicated, unlike those in prison, those with addictions, those trapped in poverty.

> They don't resent your condescension or complain that you are not politically correct; unlike widows, they don't ask you to question patriarchy; unlike orphans, they don't need money, education, or childcare; unlike aliens, they don't bring all that racial, cultural, and religious baggage that you dislike; they allow you to feel good about yourself

> without any work at creating or maintaining relationships; and when they are born, you can forget about them, because they cease to be unborn.
>
> It's almost as if, by being born, they have died to you. You can love the unborn and advocate for them without substantially challenging your own wealth, power, or privilege, without re-imagining social structures, apologizing, or making reparations to anyone. They are, in short, the perfect people to love if you want to claim you love Jesus but actually dislike people who breathe.

Prisoners? Immigrants? The sick? The poor? Widows? Orphans? All of these groups, he said, are mentioned by name in the Bible, but they all seem to be ignored because some people are so obsessed with the abortion issue.

It's a strong and determined statement, but not an unfair one. It does seem that those who describe themselves as pro-life seem to care, as I mentioned earlier, about people just before they're born and just before they die. In between, not so much. They're extremely selective in their areas of compassion, and often seem to lack it at all outside of their very select chosen areas. That, at least, is true of a great many within the movement. Indeed, by their increasing support for conservative, sometimes extreme conservative, politicians and policies, they're not merely indifferent to Christian causes but actively hostile toward them. We'll discuss this is greater depth later, but first let's look at what Jesus, and the Scriptures in general, actually say about the subject. You may be surprised.

As with homosexuality, and a number of issues that seem to so energize and enrage conservative Christians, the subject of abortion is hardly mentioned in the book they claim so dominates and shapes their lives. In other words, what is most surprising about the references to abortion in Scripture is that, generally speaking, there aren't any. And those that do exist are disturbing, not reassuring, for pro-lifers.

They'll claim as their own the command of God in Genesis that "whoever sheds the blood of a human, by a human shall that person's blood be shed; for in his own image God made humankind." So, murder is punished by murder. Which is a strict legal code for an ancient people living without police, law and order, or any form of social and prohibitive structure taken for granted in modern times. Moreover, this is about one adult killing another, and has nothing at all to do with abortion. Just before this statement, by the way, is the command that "you shall not eat flesh with its life, that is, its blood. For your own lifeblood I will surely require a reckoning: from every animal I will require it and from human beings, each one for the blood of another, I will require a reckoning for human life" — which complicates things just a little. Remember, context, context, context.

We often hear Christians with a more conservative viewpoint argue that laws and rights come from God rather than government, and while I'm convinced that the way we conduct ourselves, the way we react with and toward other people, and so many of the important moral questions we face should certainly be God-shaped in response, it's simply too facile, and dangerous, to assume that the complexities of contemporary interaction and governance are all based in holy word. It's not true, and it's not what the Bible tells us, either.

Abortion isn't new, isn't some modern idea developed by evil liberals plotting together in a room crowded with mainstream media, international financiers, and globalist heretics. Sorry to burst your conspiracy theory bubble, guys. There is ample evidence to show that it was practised in the ancient world, as far back as in Egypt sixteen centuries before the birth of Christ. What we don't find are any prohibitions against it, other than from the Assyrians, who rejected it in the strongest terms. But the Assyrians were notorious for their cruelty and butchery, and hardly a people known for offering compassion and kindness to others. It's seldom a good idea to compare anything to the Nazis, other than other Nazis, but it's difficult in this case not to think of the murderous, genocidal National Socialists who made abortion a capital offence in 1943. This, of course, applied to so-called Aryan women, and those who helped them obtain an abortion. The Nazis were determined to preserve and expand their race, whatever the cost, and their opposition to abortion was based on hatred, not heroics. I do wish that every anti-abortion activist who describes women's choice as a "holocaust" — how dare they! — would consider this fact, and empathize with those whose families were slaughtered by Hitler's maniacs. Hitler's anti-abortion maniacs. Cruel Assyrians and sadistic Nazis opposed to abortion, and both treating the born from other nations as being somehow disposable and subhuman.

Abortion is known in the Bible too, made evident when Jeremiah, writing around 600 BCE and doing his usual eponymous lamenting, curses the day he was born:

Cursed be the day
on which I was born!
The day when my mother bore me,
let it not be blessed!
Cursed be the man
who brought the news to my father, saying,
"A child is born to you, a son,"
making him very glad.
Let that man be like the cities
that the Lord overthrew without pity;
let him hear a cry in the morning
and an alarm at noon,
because he did not kill me in the womb;
so my mother would have been my grave,
and her womb forever great.
Why did I come forth from the womb
to see toil and sorrow,
and spend my days in shame?

It's a cry of deep sadness and despair, of course, but it doesn't imply prohibition or condemnation. It's not, surprisingly, a biblical reference we hear from the anti-abortion movement, but another quote from Jeremiah most certainly is. It's Jeremiah 1:5: "Before I formed you in the womb I knew you, and before you were born I consecrated you; I appointed you a prophet to the nations." This is a big one for the anti-abortion movement, and has become a virtual slogan. Largely because it's one of very few that they can find. But this has to be read within — yes — context and stated reason. Why was it said, when was it said, what does it imply or mean? Jeremiah's underlying premise is that he says he was told that he was appointed to be "a prophet to the nations." In other words, the womb reference is not a general description of one ordinary man, but a specific reference to someone set apart to do God's work. God had, we are told, predestined Jeremiah to be a prophet, and had done from the very beginning. It's a reference to a special plan for one man, rather than a general approach to biology and reproduction; a reference to the vision of God, and the importance of Jeremiah and his mission. It's also biblical hyperbole, written in a language that constantly uses rhetoric and poetry to make a particular point. The Bible isn't a novel, it's not always an easy book to understand, and Christians need to use their minds and reason, as well as their faith, when they try to understand it.

Another oft-used quote, and another that mentions the womb, is in Psalm 139:

For it was you who formed my inward parts;
you knit me together in my mother's womb.
I praise you, for I am fearfully and wonderfully made.
Wonderful are your works;
that I know very well.
My frame was not hidden from you,
when I was being made in secret,

intricately woven in the depths of the earth.
Your eyes beheld my unformed substance.
In your book were written
all the days that were formed for me,
when none of them as yet existed.

Lyrical and beautiful stuff. But, again, what is being said? God makes everything and everyone — makes people, animals, and nature. This passage is surely about God's power, and the way we should regard the creator, and doesn't say anything that is at all specific or exclusive to the fetus. The Christian belief is that God knows all, knows us, knows who and what we are. Knows, remember, the woman who is desperate, poor, young, and alone, who can't afford to have a child, was raped or abused, is terrified, has no health care, is crying out after much thought and consideration to terminate her pregnancy. Knows the goodness and purity in her heart, and the harshness of those who condemn her or who scream that her life is not as significant as what they are convinced is the baby who was "made in secret." Put simply, the ancient, biblical statement that God is all-powerful has no relevance to the rights of women over their own bodies. I believe in God, I love God, I embrace biblical teachings about God, and that's why I reject the strident position adopted by the anti-abortion movement.

The other biblical text sometimes used to oppose abortion is the sublime story in the New Testament of Elizabeth, who was the mother of John the Baptist, when she meets with Mary, the mother of Jesus. It's recounted in Luke's Gospel: "In those days Mary set out and went with haste to a Judean town in the hill country, where she entered the house of Zechariah and greeted Elizabeth. When Elizabeth heard Mary's greeting, the child leaped in her womb. And Elizabeth was filled with the Holy Spirit." It's a compelling verse for Christians, linking as it does Jesus who is the Messiah, with John who was the Baptist — who would introduce the Son of God to the world. But does it have anything at all to say about the subject of abortion? Not really. First, because it merely describes movement in the womb, and second because this is — once again — a reference to people who are not ordinary, not usual, not as the rest of us. Good Lord, this is Jesus and John the Baptist! Other people in the Bible aren't described in these terms, precisely because the Gospel writers want to make a point, not about how typical these men were but that they were the opposite. They were unique. This is a poetic illustration of the link between Jesus and John, a scriptural ballad telling of what is of the eternal, the humanizing of salvation. It's not a guide to female reproduction, and to regard it as such is to miss the entire point in such a disappointing and banal manner.

Other than this, the subject is simply not mentioned in the New Testament.

Exodus 21:22 is, however, a part of the Bible that actually does mention the fetus. "When people who are fighting injure a pregnant woman so that there is a miscarriage, and yet no further harm follows, the one responsible shall be fined what the woman's husband demands, paying as much as the judges determine. If any harm follows, then you shall give life for life, eye for eye, tooth for tooth, hand for hand, foot for foot, burn for burn, wound for wound, stripe for stripe." This is fascinating, because it outlines specific punishments for specific crimes. If a woman is hurt in a struggle and then has a miscarriage, the penalty is a fine, a mere financial payment. But if there is further harm, likely meaning the woman has long-term and serious injuries or even dies, then the culprit could be killed. In other words, the well-being or life of the woman, the mother, is of much greater significance and importance than that of her unborn child.

The Greek translation of this passage is also worth considering, as early Christians usually read their Scriptures in Greek. This tells us something a little different. "If two men fight and strike a pregnant woman and her child comes out not fully formed, he (the striker) will be forced to pay a penalty. But if it is fully formed, he shall give life for life." So, if a fully formed baby is killed, the penalty is death, but in earlier stages of development the punishment is still a mere fine. And this, remember, is for what is effectively an abortion against the will of the mother, caused in violence and during criminality. It contains no restriction on the woman's own choice and actions. The Mishnah, a collection of Jewish laws based on oral tradition, and written around two hundred years after Jesus, permits abortion if the pregnancy is difficult, meaning that the life and well-being of the mother are far more significant than the life of the fetus.

Numbers 5, in the Old Testament, has something to say about the subject. It makes for very difficult reading to modern audiences, as does so much contained in the codes and laws of the early Jewish people — as we saw in the chapter that discussed homosexuality. It's why it's so necessary to have a sense of interpretation and understanding, and so dangerous to try to exploit isolated verses to make a political point, especially thousands of years after the book was written. This section discusses the treatment of a wife who is suspected of adultery, of betraying her husband. The priest is directed to say,

> "But if you have gone astray while under your husband's authority, if you have defiled yourself and some man other than your husband has had intercourse with you," – let the priest make the woman take the oath of the curse and say to the woman – "the Lord make you an execration and an oath among your people, when the Lord makes your uterus drop, your womb discharge; now may this water that brings the curse enter your bowels and make your womb discharge, your uterus drop!" And the woman shall say, "Amen. Amen."

There have been all sorts of readings down the centuries, but the instruction seems to call for a jealous husband to take his poor wife to the priest, the judge, and if her pregnancy is thought to be the result of an affair with another man, she is obliged to drink what many modern scholars regard as an abortion-inducing concoction. The story is quite obviously of its era and place, but does rather contradict the anti-choice argument that the biblical commandment "You shall not murder" somehow applies to abortion. It clearly doesn't, unless God is in the habit of frequent self-contradiction. I can't pretend that it's pleasing to discuss passages like this, that seem so brutal and severe, but when anti-choice protesters tell their opponents, "Look, it's there in the Bible," I'm afraid they're right. It is indeed in the Bible. Which is why they need to understand their Bibles properly.

Of course, if these opponents of abortion were genuinely to live by this commandment that we must never kill, they would oppose wars, the military, the death penalty, and policies that lead directly to poverty, hunger, ill health, and death. To the contrary, the anti-abortion movement has become increasingly politically conservative over the years — it was, for example, one of the bulwarks of the Donald Trump presidency — and tends to be solidly behind the military and an aggressive foreign policy. It's usually supportive of the death penalty, as well. Contradiction and inconsistency. Abortion isn't murder, murder is murder. Abortion isn't a holocaust, the Holocaust was the Holocaust. And a woman's right to choose is a woman's right to choose. That's the rebel Christ approach.

In terms of the Bible, that is about it. We can dig away at some other scriptural references to try to justify various positions on this issue but they're all somewhat tenuous and none of them make an ironclad argument. It's not that the Bible demands abortion rights, more that it simply doesn't have anything pertinent to say about the subject. Women's choice is a central part of the development of gender equality, social liberation, and scientific progress, and it's downright unbiblical to try to twist Scripture to argue against it.

It's certainly not an easy subject, and anybody, on either side of this issue, who claims that every question has been answered and every challenge solved is being disingenuous at best. I've never met anybody who claims that abortion is good or desirable, but then neither would they argue that any form of surgery or medical intervention is good or desirable. It's necessary, life-changing, life-saving, but not in itself something to be wanted. The matter is further complicated in the case of abortion, because the "potential" for life certainly exists. Sometimes, though rarely, the reasons for termination are controversial, especially when they involve disability or gender. But these are not the underlying reasons for abortion, and the solution is not to restrict women's choice but to build societies where those with disabilities do not face discrimination and insult, and where gender equality is the absolute norm. As for late-term abortions, so often used as a debating point, an interesting exchange took place during the 2020 presidential election campaign, between U.S. secretary of transportation and former mayor of South Bend, Indiana, Pete Buttigieg, and Fox News's Chris Wallace. The journalist asked the politician, "Do you believe, at any point in pregnancy, whether it's at six weeks or eight weeks or twenty-four weeks or whenever, that there should be any limit on a woman's right to have an abortion?" Buttigieg answered, "I think the dialogue has gotten so caught up on where you draw the line that we've gotten away from the fundamental question of who gets to draw the line, and I trust women to draw the line when it's their own health."

Wallace continued, asking if Buttigieg, a man of devout Christian faith, was comfortable with late-term abortions, as more than six thousand women have third-trimester abortions each year. Buttiegieg replied,

> That's right, representing one percent of cases. So let's put ourselves in the shoes of a woman in that situation. If it's that late in your pregnancy, then almost by definition, you've been expecting to carry it to term. We're talking about women who have perhaps chosen a name. Women who have purchased a crib, families that then get the most devastating medical news of their lifetime, something about

> the health or the life of the mother or viability of the pregnancy that forces them to make an impossible, unthinkable choice. And the bottom line is as horrible as that choice is, that woman, that family may seek spiritual guidance, they may seek medical guidance, but that decision is not going to be made any better, medically or morally, because the government is dictating how that decision should be made.

I don't think I've ever heard it as succinctly and responsibly expressed. In a perfect world, that would end the controversy about late-term abortions. We don't live in a perfect world.

Reluctant as I am to say it, experience leads me to conclude that the anti-abortion movement certainly doesn't always indicate a Christ-based love for others. A woman who visits an abortion clinic is likely to be deeply apprehensive, maybe even terrified. No one in such a situation should have to cope with fundamentalist fanatics screaming at her for obtaining a legal and necessary medical procedure. In any free and civilized society, those who oppose abortion have a sacred right to their point of view. And in any free and civilized society, women have the right to control their bodies without being browbeaten by angry zealots. As a journalist, I've reported on several such demonstrations; it's not something I can recommend. Those who protest outside abortion clinics tend to come from the right-wing fringes of Christianity, and their archconservative views go far beyond abortion; some of the opinions they express about, for example, the LGBTQ2 community are quite terrifying. I've heard the rants, seen the faces, been on the receiving end of the insults.

The humiliation and degradation inflicted on women outside clinics is genuinely shocking. I've watched protesters howling at vulnerable women walking into clinics, calling them "murderers" and predicting that "God will not forgive" them. Even the quiet ones hold up accusatory placards or plead with young women "not to kill your baby." Two high-profile female anti-abortion activists in

Toronto, for example, are routinely arrested for breaking the city's no-protest zones around abortion clinics, prompting conservative columnists to complain that they will eventually spend more time in prison than various killers and rapists. Maybe that's true. If so, it's regrettable, but it's not the point. For many of these protesters, getting arrested is exactly what they want. It's not about the women in the clinic, not about the fetus, and certainly not about the rebel Christ.

Then there are the people who insist on distributing millions of leaflets showing graphic, bloody pictures of abortions, even putting them through the front doors of private homes when they know that children will see them. But for them the cause is everything, and abortion is always wrong, even in cases of rape, incest, or a threat to the life of the mother. While they claim to be non-violent, it's difficult to be convinced. Violence has certainly taken place, and it's included kidnapping, assault, attempted murder, murder, arson, bombings, and stalking. Anti-abortion extremists are considered a domestic terrorist threat by the Department of Justice in the United States, where most of the incidents occur. There have also been attacks in Australia, New Zealand, Canada, and elsewhere.

In the U.S., at least eleven people involved in providing abortion services, including four doctors, two clinic employees, a security guard, and a police officer, have been murdered. As recently as late November 2015 in Colorado Springs, a shooting at Planned Parenthood killed three people and injured several others. The suspect described himself as a "warrior for the babies." In 2001 an extremist named Clayton Waagner mailed hoax letters containing white powder to more than 550 abortion clinics, claiming that these were anthrax attacks.

Even in allegedly peaceful and moderate Canada it happens. In 1992, Dr. Henry Morgentaler's clinic in Toronto was hit by a firebomb, following several less-successful arson attacks. Morgentaler championed the cause of women's reproductive rights in the country, was repeatedly threatened with violence and even murder, and was sometimes physically attacked. In 1997, Manitoba doctor Jack

Fainman — an obstetrician who performed abortions — was shot by a sniper as he sat in his living room. Winnipeg police called the sniper-style attack "terrorism against doctors." He survived, but his injuries meant that he could never work as a doctor again. This gruesome behaviour is hardly consistent with a life ethic, and certainly not with Christian teaching. A violence, an ugliness, and an intolerance has crept into the anti-abortion movement, and the indications are that these emotions and attitudes are becoming worse rather than the opposite.

It all seems so manufactured, so rooted in something far outside of the Gospel narrative. Also, quite recent. As recently as 1968, for example, a meeting held by the Christian Medical Society and the highly influential evangelical magazine *Christianity Today* concluded that abortion had to be considered in the light of "individual health, family welfare, and social responsibility" and the organizers refused to describe abortion as sinful. Three years later the Southern Baptist Convention, perhaps the most important conservative denomination in North America, passed a resolution calling on "Southern Baptists to work for legislation that will allow the possibility of abortion under such conditions as rape, incest, clear evidence of severe fetal deformity, and carefully ascertained evidence of the likelihood of damage to the emotional, mental, and physical health of the mother." The reference to the emotional, mental, and physical health of the woman carrying the fetus leaves the door wide open to abortion rights. Meaning that the exponential growth between evangelical Christianity and a radical opposition to abortion does seem to be extremely short-lived.

It's part of the emerging parallel between political and religious conservatism, used as a way to mobilize evangelical Christians to work in favour of numerous other right-wing positions, and to support various conservative political parties. In the U.S., Republican politicians may have any number of views on different issues, but opposition to abortion has become almost a sacrament in the catechism of reaction. It gives the impression of being far more about politics than about life or faith.

The Roman Catholic position is a little different but, with all due respect, we are discussing an institution that remains the largest and most powerful patriarchy in the world. I realize that the term *patriarchy* is used quite often, perhaps too often today, but it applies supremely to a body where only men can be deacons, priests, bishops, cardinals, or popes; where so many of the women who are revered are virgins and nuns; where the female experience is ignored, or interpreted in such a falsely pious manner as to make it the stuff of cartoon fantasy. There are countless genuinely noble people in the Catholic Church, but the teaching that sexual activity is designed solely for procreation, that contraception is a sin, and the near obsession with sexuality and sex does make it difficult to accept Catholic teachings about abortion. Then, tragically, there is the agonizing record of the church regarding the rape of children by priests, and the concerted attempts at the highest levels to obfuscate and deny the crimes and protect the culprits.

Better, surely, to listen to Roman Catholic nun Sister Joan Chittister, a hero of reality in a religious culture that often rejects it. "I do not believe that just because you're opposed to abortion, that that makes you pro-life. In fact, I think in many cases, your morality is deeply lacking if all you want is a child born but not a child fed, not a child educated, not a child housed. And why would I think that you don't? Because you don't want any tax money to go there. That's not pro-life. That's pro-birth. We need a much broader conversation on what the morality of pro-life is."

In all of the Christian opposition to abortion there is a strong element of control, a notion that women don't merit autonomy, and are vessels and vehicles for children. They have a duty to be mothers, not the right to be independent beings with their own right to choose. That's not biblical, that's certainly not Jesus. Apart from the obvious offensiveness of it all, it's just not biblical. Women were the first to see the resurrected Christ, and were not believed by the frightened men who cowered in upper rooms and in hiding. The women of the New

Testament and the apostolic Church — such as Prisca, Lydia, Phoebe, Chloe, Nympha — are central to the Christian story. A woman, Mary his mother, tells Jesus to perform his first miracle, the turning of water into wine. Mary, who questions an angel; Mary, who is so concerned about Jesus's state of mind during his ministry; Mary, who is at the cross when so many others have run away; Mary, who says,

He has shown strength with his arm;
he has scattered the proud in the thoughts of their hearts.
He has brought down the powerful from their thrones,
and lifted up the lowly;
he has filled the hungry with good things,
and sent the rich away empty.

Jesus is about the humanity and equality of all of us, he is about the brave new world that is light and bright. This magnificent rebel shouldn't be reduced to a poster or a slogan used to hurt half of the world's population, and to force them into powerlessness and degradation.

Which leads us back to what the United Methodist pastor in Alabama said at the beginning of the chapter. Let's go further. The anti-abortion movement has lost, if it had it in the first place, the right to describe itself as pro-life. Their cause is birth, not life. Or, to be more blunt, conception rather than birth; because those in the U.S. give little support to socialized medicine and often strongly oppose it. That leaves poor and marginalized mothers, and their pregnancies, in a very dangerous place. If opponents of abortion seriously cared about the birth of the child and the life of the mother, they would want struggling women to have access to doctors and to constant medical care. Once conception takes place, however, interest seems to evaporate. More than this, there are various ways that abortion rates could drop, as have been proved in many countries. Not by criminalizing abortion. All that does is remove women's rights, allow wealthier women to simply travel to other states or countries to have abortions, and force poor women into further and deeper poverty and despair and make them seek out dangerous backstreet procedures. No, if anti-abortionists genuinely wanted rates to drop, they would support freely available contraception, good and modern sex education in all schools, gender equality, a war on poverty, publicly funded and freely available daycare, and enforced financial support from divorced fathers. But they don't.

Let's just take one of those issues: sex education. It has been proven to make young people more aware of what sex means, and that awareness leads to greater responsibility. It reduces the numbers of unwanted pregnancies and, as a direct consequence, reduces rates of abortion. Yet I've never met or heard of a leading anti-abortion activist who supports modern, thorough, and realistic sex education in schools. On the contrary, they regard it as dangerous intervention by the state, or as somehow an attempt to pervert their children and to take away parental responsibility. But the direct alternative to sex education in school isn't parental instruction but the internet, where all sorts of misinformation can be found. Christian parents are hardly renowned for their willingness to broach these issues with their children, much less provide the open and honest talk that is needed. By sparing their sons and daughters an updated sexual education, and maybe even encouraging them to think sex is too lurid to be spoken about, parents risk shaming their children into thinking that the act is wrong. That doesn't stop sex occurring, but increases the chances of it being secret, guilt-ridden, and unprotected.

Jesus isn't shame or guilt, isn't about hating pleasure and love.

And if anything, the various curricula are designed to reduce promiscuity and to teach young girls in particular that they have control over what they do with their bodies. The idea of self-worth permeates sex education, and dignity is a crucial element in sexual health. It empowers consent and leads to far more mature relationships. In reality, sex-ed lessons are fairly clinical, and even numbingly cold. As one sex-ed teacher told me, "Sexy this is not. Many of the kids are embarrassed, and a lot of them think it's funny or, the word I hear most, *gross*." Gross or not, it's designed to remove that stigma. Vancouver-based nurse Meg Hickling, who has worked in sex ed for more than twenty-five years, says that "there are thousands of studies all over the world that show that the earlier you start, the healthier the children are going to be and the easier it is for them to make good, informed decisions for themselves." If children have the vocabulary, self-confidence, and educational tools, they are far less likely to cause a pregnancy, or to become pregnant when they do not intend to be.

An aside. The most popular and successful comment I ever made on Twitter concerned this issue. "I sympathize with those who fear that sex ed will sexualize kids. Our youngest studied WWI on a Monday; by Friday he'd invaded Belgium." There were an extraordinary 240,000 "likes," but the angry responses — and there were a number — were quite extraordinary, many if not most of them from Christian anti-abortion types convinced that sex ed would destroy everything they held sacred and, naturally, lead to more abortions. "But Jesus said, 'Suffer little children.'" It doesn't quite mean that, of course, but you get the point.

A personal story. In 2019, I went to see a controversial anti-abortion movie called *Unplanned*. It was receiving a great deal of publicity, and I didn't go for a night's entertainment but as a journalistic exercise. It was truly appalling. The acting was wooden, the plot was cliché upon caricature, the depiction of abortion providers cartoonish, and it was all wrapped up in gory and ghoulish scenes of the blood-soaked hands of evil liberals and snarling feminists.

It was partly financed by the now rather well-known pillow manufacturer Mike Lindell, who once said that Donald Trump was "the greatest president in history ... chosen by God," and was one of Trump's few remaining supporters in the final days of the man's disastrous presidency — and this was after the murderous and treasonous attack on the Capitol Building conducted by pro-Trump extremists. A pillow would have helped me when I watched the movie, but not those around me. Goodness, they were engaged! They cried, screamed, and prayed. There was palpable anger, and a cheering and clapping when the movie ended.

That reaction is important to note because, as we have seen, abortion medics have been attacked and killed, and many of those Trump zealots who smashed their way into the seat of U.S. government in January 2021 were militant opponents of abortion, as was proved by their statements and writings. So while there is no doubt that the movie is raw, clumsy, and didactic, it does succeed in creating an atmosphere of fear and anger. It rallies the troops, so to speak.

The story of *Unplanned* concerns anti-abortion activist Abby Johnson, on whose memoir the movie is based. Many medical experts have questioned her book and the subsequent film, but testimony from doctors has never been an obstacle for the anti-abortion movement. Abby glides from being a supporter of choice and from working in a clinic to becoming a fierce opponent of abortion. It's all about profit and money, the movie insists, and even if it wasn't, a fetus can feel pain. Let's just hope then that no unborn child ever has to sit through this agonizing nonsense. It concludes with the local Planned Parenthood in Texas being closed, and Abby goes on to have lots of children and become a Roman Catholic. The clinic in question actually did have to close, as have others in conservative states in the U.S. Leaving women to raise their children in poverty, because most of the states restricting abortion rights are also the most resistant to increased welfare payments, public medicine, racial equality, and education opportunities.

Back to my evening out. When the movie ended the lights went on and the audience began to look around and to speak to each other. Some of them were comforting their friends, who were in tears. As eyes focused and as people stood up, I was noticed, because in parts of Canada I am known as someone who once opposed abortion, but then embraced a more Christian approach to the subject. Pockets of people began to quite clearly point at me and then to whisper to those sitting close to them. There was no violence, but a lot of rather unpleasant stares. Then, as I got up and started to leave, a woman shouted from the middle rows, "Their blood is on your head, sir, their deaths are at your hands." I considered a response, but instead just smiled and continued my way out of the theatre. Abby Johnson herself later wrote to me, explaining kindly that "I'm not going to read what you wrote, but I do appreciate that you are helping us to get the word out about this film! Any PR is good PR!" Well, that's nice.

The argument, of course, doesn't end with abortion. If someone is committed to the dignity of life, they should be concerned with it at every stage, and not just with the artificial construct of the "unborn."

What I've always found so baffling about the conservative Christian position is that it's so concerned to keep people alive when they actually want to put an end to their lives because of insurmountable suffering. The issue of assisted dying. Opposition, or at least concern, goes well beyond the conservative wing of the church, but it's Christians who lead the charge against any progress in this area. Increasingly, however, surveys reveal that the majority of people believe in a controlled, supervised, and extremely limited form of assisted dying for people who are experiencing dreadful suffering, and whose death is close and will be otherwise painful and likely isolated. But Christian conservatives see this is as an attack upon their faith, and, rather like their opposition to abortion rights and equal marriage, are fighting tenaciously to oppose legislation that might support such a policy. In fact, it's become one of the key issues for many churches.

The language is important here. It's not "suicide" or "compassionate homicide." It's a highly skilled and caring medical system helping a terminally ill person in full control of their wits to end their life just a little before it otherwise would, surrounded by their loved ones, and before the agony and terror become too much to tolerate. What is imperative to understand is that the alternative to assisted dying is not living. The alternative to assisted dying is unassisted dying. That means dying in pain, anguish, and often totally alone, because that death — that thief in the night — can come at any time.

This isn't about encouraging death or, as has been suggested, a death cult or murder panels, but rather listening to someone who merely asks for control over their own body and their own fate. Nor is it necessarily about quality of life, which is a phrase far too often exploited for political ends. Disability, for example, does not indicate lack of quality. Daily struggle does not mean a lack of quality. And age certainly does not mean that quality is lacking. We need to invest far more money into caring for the elderly and into palliative care, and to make sure that every possibility is open to people, achieved by a massive sharing of the public purse, that should be supported by all Christians. At the moment, even in countries that enjoy socialized medicine, the percentage of money injected into this area of medical and social care simply isn't sufficient. We also need to work to change cultural norms so that we respect rather than reject the elderly, and see them as mansions of wisdom and grace, not as decaying old buildings that have served their purpose.

Consider what it would be like if you knew that you had months or perhaps even a year left to live, and that very soon the pain, in spite of medication, would be so overwhelming that you would need to be made almost comatose so as not to feel anything. Or that a neurological disease had taken hold and you knew that before long your muscles would waste away, and that while the mind was still active, the body would eventually drown in its own fluids. The daily reality of people choosing the time of their death has nothing to do with movie romance or pious flippancy, but a devout wish to say goodbye to friends and family, and to leave with a certain degree of self-respect and control before the person is no more, even though the body still partly functions. The idea that medical staff are anxious to end people's lives, or indifferent to their suffering and the pain of their families, is as insulting as it is ludicrous. Any system that is developed to respond to all this has to be heavily regulated, and led by doctors who, contrary to what the extremists say, have dedicated their lives to making people well and keeping them alive.

There is a great deal of ignorance about all this, and far too many achingly banal comments about "slippery slopes" and the like. I have to wonder, how many of these people have sat with an ailing loved one and heard them beg and plead to be permitted to go just a little early, while they can still grasp the love and the positive experience that their life has been? Personal story. My dad served in Bomber Command in the Second World War. He had been a champion amateur boxer, raised two children, worked hard all of his life, and loved his wife, my mum. He knew after his second stroke, and the returned cancer, that it was over, that he had little time left, and that it would be ghastly. He wanted to go. He turned his head to me one day and mouthed a few words that will always remain private. I was powerless, of course, and when I spoke to the doctor — a wonderful, caring, Christian woman — she simply held my arm and said nothing. The law didn't permit her to intervene, and as a result my dear father's suffering lasted longer than it should have. His death was not a good one, and he deserved so much better.

Finally, the challenge of capital punishment, the death penalty, because it's very much a life issue. The wealthy and middle class are far more likely to have access to lawyers who can better defend them, and know the best procedures and methods to avoid execution; they are generally better treated by the judicial system, and by judges and juries; and because they are not caught up in circles of poverty and deprivation they are less likely to offend, or be thought to have offended, in the first place.

Those Christians who defend the killing of offenders usually base their arguments on the Old Testament, but as we've seen throughout the book, that position has to be treated with enormous care and consideration. The Hebrew Scriptures are a vital part of the Christian story, but — again — much of what they demand is of a particular era and of a particular people. They are often legal rather than moral codes, and simply don't apply to the modern age. They have nothing to say about contemporary conditions or the contemporary conversation. Nor am I sure that those making these arguments have read the entire book. The book of Deuteronomy, for example, says that two or three witnesses are required before the death penalty can be applied. Ezekiel writes: "If he has a son who is violent, a shedder of blood, who does any of these things (though his father does none of them), who eats upon the mountains, defiles his neighbor's wife, oppresses the poor and needy, commits robbery, does not restore the pledge, lifts up his eyes to the idols, commits abomination, takes advance or accrued interest; shall he then live? He shall not. He has done all these abominable things; he shall surely die; his blood shall be upon himself."

That's a pretty long and extensive list, and much as I sometimes feel a little upset at the interest rates changed by banks and credit card companies, I wouldn't want all of those nice and well-meaning people to be slaughtered.

Then comes Jesus, who would eventually face a show trial at the hands of people who had already made up their minds about his fate, had no sense of true justice, and enjoyed power over the powerless. He would be condemned and he would be executed. During his ministry he directly addressed this issue, in the Gospel of Matthew. "You have heard that it was said, 'An eye for an eye and a tooth for a tooth.' But I say to you, Do not resist an evildoer. But if anyone strikes you on the right cheek, turn the other also; and if anyone wants to sue you and take your coat, give your cloak as well; and if anyone forces you to go one mile, go also the second mile. Give to everyone who begs from you, and do not refuse anyone who wants to borrow from you."

First of all, the eye-for-an-eye approach may not be quite what it seems. It's often quoted to justify some sort of revenge, or in this case the death penalty, but may well have been a command to limit a response, to act in proportion to a crime committed. In other words, an eye for an eye rather than a life for an eye. Even so, Jesus gives the world a new way forward, as he does with so much in his teaching. Also, when Jesus deals with the crowd who want to stone the woman caught in adultery — a scene we've already discussed — he not only exposes their hypocrisy, and rejects legalism, but he's also preventing an execution. Stoning was not only a means of punishment and humiliation, but a standard method of execution. That woman would have been killed, judicially and according to the law. When, again in Matthew, Jesus says, "Go and learn what this means, 'I desire mercy, not sacrifice,'" he is insisting that those who wish to follow him grasp the loving nature of this new covenant. Rebel against the darkness of which we are all capable.

The death penalty kills innocent people. That is a fact so well documented that it's unnecessary to discuss it any further here. In some countries it's used as a means of political oppression, and the activities of regimes in Iran, China, and elsewhere are notorious. But it also ends the lives of people who have indeed committed terrible crimes. Yet these are often men and women who are mentally challenged, or were in the grip of an addiction, or have stories that would make us weep. Not all though. There are those who were in full control of their actions, but out of sadism, or indifference toward others, or greed, or lust, murdered someone, faced a fair trial, and were rightly convicted. There are all sorts of arguments as to why the death penalty is still unacceptable, but this isn't a secular book. No clear, honest reading of the Gospel would lead us to conclude that Jesus would smile at the idea of a gas chamber, a fatal injection, or an electric chair. If I lost a loved one to murder my immediate, visceral response would likely be to want the culprit killed. I understand that, I'm honest about it. My pain and my loss would cry out for revenge. The rebel Christ asks us to go beyond the visceral and the immediate, to pass over revenge, and to grasp something better and finer. More Christian.

Pope Francis has long opposed capital punishment, but in 2015 offered his most concrete rejection yet. He called it "inadmissible, no matter how serious the crime committed." He went on, "It is an offence against the inviolability of life and the dignity of the human person, which contradicts God's plan for man and society, and his merciful justice, and impedes the penalty from fulfilling any just objective. It does not render justice to the victims, but rather fosters vengeance." And, "When the death penalty is applied, it is not for a current act of aggression, but rather for an act committed in the past. It is also applied to persons whose current ability to cause harm is not current, as it has been neutralized — they are already deprived of their liberty." That's a remarkable and Christ-filled statement.

So many double standards and inconsistencies, so much unnecessary pain and suffering, so little point. The belief that from the moment of conception a complete human being exists is, whatever some might hope or want, not a scientific or rational belief. It's not even a theory that many Christians support. The Bible, if it tells us anything about this subject, suggests that life begins at the first breath, in other words after a birth, and that babies aren't considered fully worthy until they're a month old. The rebel Christ tells us to listen, to think, and to reflect on how others feel. The rebel Christ tells us not to judge but to love, and to try to make the world better and more equitable for everybody, everywhere.

A Last Word

C.S. Lewis, one of the greatest communicators of the Christian message in modern times, has been a lasting influence on my life, ever since *The Lion, the Witch, and the Wardrobe* was read to me by my teacher when I was five years old. The phrase "Onward and Upward! To Narnia and the North!" is from his children's novel *The Horse and His Boy*, another in the Narnia series. It applies so powerfully to the future of the church. We move on, and we move up — on to a closer relationship with Jesus and an understanding of his purpose, and up a higher challenge of living out the Gospel as it deserves.

I was privileged to know Walter Hooper, who was friend and secretary to Lewis in 1963, in the final months of the author's life. Walter always insisted that those more conservative evangelicals who had adopted Lewis as a form of saint had often got the man badly wrong. "He wasn't political as such, but he lived the Gospel ideas of love, charity, and kindness," explained Walter. "I remember when he gave some money to a beggar on the street, and was criticized, told that the man would only spend it on drink. 'Well,' said Lewis, 'that's exactly what I would have spent it on!' That was typical of the man. He tried to look at the world anew, from a different angle, from the point of view of the victim, the people often written out of the picture and the story."

That "looking at the world anew" is basic Gospel teaching. It's not always easy, of course, and wasn't supposed to be. Following the rebel Christ isn't some convenient aid to modern living but a transforming commitment to a different life. There are no mantras or manuals, no online courses that will make everything pleasing and fulfilling. Christ asks for struggle and work, sacrifice and effort. We follow out of love and out of belief, and we follow because it reaches the point where we can do no other. Following that path, however, is a daily challenge because we're so often limited by our own experience and environment, by what we have known and with what we feel familiar.

So many deserve better. Pray God — and I use the name of the deity purposely — we will all come to our senses on this, and approach such a delicate issue with compassion rather than ideology. It is not, whatever others might suggest, blasphemous to challenge long-held church opinions with an informed and prayerful Christian disagreement. The rebel Christ told us that throughout his ministry. Blasphemy is offending God, and we offend God by remaining silent in the face of pain and injustice, and on that note I want to speak briefly about the issue of blasphemy, because I confidently expect some of my more conservative co-religionists to apply that accusation to this book. I don't matter, but the reputation of Christianity most certainly does.

Blasphemy became an issue once again in Ireland at the start of 2021 when the national broadcaster RTÉ apologized after protests sparked by a television comedy sketch that depicted God as a rapist. A show on New Year's Eve had featured a twenty-three-second satirical news report naming God in a sexual harassment scandal. "The five-billion-year-old stood accused of forcing himself on a young Middle Eastern migrant and allegedly impregnating her against her will, before being sentenced to two years in prison, with the last twenty-four months suspended," it announced. "Following the news, movie producer Harvey Weinstein requested a retrial in Ireland."

Cue more than a thousand complaints; condemnation by the country's primate, archbishop Eamon Martin; and RTÉ responding that it recognized "that matters which can cause offence naturally differ from person to person, within comedy and satire in particular. Having reviewed the feedback and complaints received up to this point, RTÉ wishes to apologize to those who were offended by the segment." The "those who were offended" defence is pretty common these days, and means relatively little, but it does expose that while formal blasphemy may be a rare concept in the contemporary western world, it still features in popular consciousness. The last actual prosecution in Ireland was back in 1855 when a priest accidentally burned a Bible — well, it can happen to the best of us. More recently, in 2017, Stephen Fry was briefly investigated by the Irish police on charges of blasphemy. The case was based on remarks he'd made on Irish television two years earlier and, if convicted, Fry could have faced a fine of €25,000.

The cops couldn't find enough evidence to continue the investigation — and I'm sure didn't try very hard — much to the chagrin of Fry, who would have liked nothing more than a good old blasphemy trial. What he actually said, however, is worth noting. Asked how he would respond if God did in fact exist and he met him after death, he replied: "How dare you create a world in which there is such misery that is not our fault? It's not right. It's utterly, utterly evil. Why should I respect a capricious, mean-minded, stupid god who creates a world which is so full of injustice and pain?"

He continued: "Because the god who created this universe, if it was created by god, is quite clearly a maniac, an utter maniac, totally selfish. We have to spend our lives on our knees thanking him. What kind of god would do that?" Which is a wonderful, astute question to ask, and something that as a cleric I'd use as a starting point for a systematic theology or apologetics class, if they were ever sufficiently foolish to let me teach in a seminary. The point is that I don't have to agree with Fry — who was, by the way, a kind and encouraging friend to me during my journey toward ordination — to respect the sentiment and the challenge. Faith is a dialogue, and tough and painful questions can't be strangled or ignored simply because they are difficult. That way is the road to oppression, bigotry, and intolerance. Christ challenged and prodded, even provoked, all the time.

Insult for its own sake is childish and banal, but strong words to make an argument or to oppose a creed — satirical or otherwise — are not only acceptable but also absolutely vital in a healthy democracy. Those social media atheists who moan on about sky-fairies and all Christians being stupid are simply dull. But intelligent and informed debate between believer and non-believer, divine thesis and antithesis, should strengthen and refine a faith that is authentic and vibrant. It's difficult to forget even now the uproar over *Monty Python's Life of Brian* in 1979. If the film did have a point to make, apart from being simply funny and entertaining, it was that the loving and pure message of Jesus was forgotten in the rush to embrace pointless detail and pedantic observance. It should have been sacrilegious only to Pharisees, but that didn't stop it being banned in cinemas, and from various zealots and frauds denouncing it all over the media. I saw more of the real, honest, believable rebel Christ in that film than in any number of episodes of *Touched by an Angel*!

What was said on Irish television was brief, pithy, and making a statement about the nature of God and humanity, one that shouldn't worry any Christian who understands the true nature of the annunciation. If it does, tough. Far, far more agonizing is the child-abuse horror that permeated the Roman Catholic Church and is still being unwrapped. Far, far more agonizing is the galloping homophobia and the obsession with contraception and women's choice that still dominate so much of Christian discourse. They do far more harm to the church than any amount of comedy. Blasphemy against Jesus and the Gospels does exist, but it comes from fundamentalists and literalists who so distort the original message of the gentle rabbi Yeshua. It came, for example, from those people we spoke of at the start of the book who stormed the Capitol Building in Washington, D.C., waving Christian placards and wearing shirts emblazoned with "Jesus Saves." The public square in secular society should have no special protection for religious faith. All I ask is that it should have no particular animus, either. Satirize all you want, but let us respond and participate without benefit of clergy, or with prejudice against believers. If the church acted as a church, if Christians acted as Christians, if followers of Jesus acted as followers of Jesus, not only would the world be an extremely different place, but organized Christianity would be compelling, even irresistible, to myriad people.

It's something I pray for daily, and while I made it clear that this book isn't a work of apologetics, I do want to discuss prayer, so as to perhaps clarify the subject for those who think that Jesus sounds far more appealing than they might have originally thought, but they can't accept the idea of communicating with God. Prayer should be at the centre of all Christian relationships. But prayer can also be abused, misunderstood, and lost. In early November 2017, for example, as worshippers at First Baptist Church in Sutherland Springs, Texas, settled into their regular Sunday service, a twenty-six-year-old man named Devin Patrick Kelley opened fire. By the end of the slaughter, twenty-six people in the congregation were dead, and many others horribly wounded. One family alone, the Holcombes, lost eight members. Media reaction was immediate, with journalists and politicians exclaiming that the horror was "unimaginable." In fact, it was entirely imaginable, in that such horrors have happened so many times before and, alas, will surely happen again.

We heard repeatedly that people were "praying" for the victims, and that their "thoughts and prayers" were with them. A number of those announcements came from Republican politicians who receive significant donations and support from the National Rifle Association, and who repeatedly vote against any form of meaningful gun control. So, on the one hand they were apparently chatting away to God about how awful it all was, while simultaneously making sure any future mass murderer would have access to deadly weapons. It does rather shake one's faith in the integrity of those who pray, and even in prayer itself. It shouldn't, but it does.

I'm a Christian and I pray — morning, noon, and night. I pray silently as I walk to the subway, pray formally during set offices expected of serious Anglicans. I pray even in stressful public situations and when I feel slightly awkward doing so. I wasn't raised in a religious family and only started to pray when I became a Christian in the mid-1980s, but now I could no more not pray than not eat. And rather like food, prayer often delights me, sometimes leaves me disappointed, but always nourishes me. But we live in a time when prayer has often been stripped of that nourishment, its substance watered down until the act seems largely meaningless and banal, rather like a handshake or a casual "How are you?" It's even used as an emotional weapon: ostentatious Christians on social media explaining that they will "pray for you," the subtext being that you are so wrong and almost certainly damned. Along with politicians, we have scores of movie actors and sports stars who regularly tell us that they are praying for peace, happiness, good weather, and even a win against a rival. Then there are the onlookers at murder scenes, especially when a child is involved. They hold up posters announcing that they are praying, and always seem to find a television reporter who will nod sympathetically as they tell the world they are praying for the angel now in heaven and praying that the swine who committed the crime will suffer for eternity.

There are, of course, many forms of prayer, just as there are many forms of religion, and many forms of religious people. Prayer is mutable, fluid, and various. The first and most central reality is that prayer is far more about changing oneself than about about pressuring God into action. Because of its intimate nature, we're at our most honest in prayer, assuming in a great thrust of trust that we can say and admit anything — odd, in that we only pray if we believe God can hear, yet we seem to not mind, not be embarrassed, by what is heard. While we do make requests, we more often confess to what we really are, who we really are. That's an incredibly difficult and challenging exercise, and something rarely attempted in modern, secular society. The catharsis, if genuine, is powerful. It's of course inevitable that we also ask for things; that's part of the human condition, and beating ourselves up for it is self-defeating. But to reduce prayer to an empty response to difficult and even terrifying situations, or to a supernatural shopping list, is to misunderstand the act itself.

Jesus tells us that prayer is about letting go, allowing, accepting. In a way, it's a profound acquiescence, a sometimes reluctant acceptance that we may not know what is best and that there is someone above and beyond us. The supreme paradox that is Christianity — in defeat is victory, and in death is life — is profoundly contrary to the triumphalist, proud, and sectarian Christianity we hear so often from religious conservatives. The correlative of that paradox — the abandonment of the self, the ego — is also about as heretical as it gets in the modern age, this era of the "me" as the epicentre of all that is good and precious. Prayer is in some ways the expunging of the individual, allowing us to become something less defined, to be part of a spiritual collective.

That may sound New Age or strange; but then, prayer is nothing if not strange. When I pray I never feel alone, even though I am usually physically isolated. I feel a link to others, that I am part of a spiritual body that is not only Christian but of all faiths. Here we all are, often oceans apart and speaking different languages, but united by a belief that many other people reject as foolish or condemn as naive or worse. Sitting alone in my study at prayer, I feel part of a crowd. Not the "in" crowd, of course, but the right crowd. The rebel Christ crowd.

Nothing about this is tangible or crisp; God doesn't really do rational and linear, which is why a literal reading of the Bible gets people into such trouble. Within that Bible there is invincible wisdom and truth — Gospel truth, if you like — but we are not robotic followers: we are thinking, questioning men and women trying to find paths of goodness. That's why prayer is so important. It helps us find the prism of faith and filter of intellect through which we can understand the meaning of texts written so long ago. Fundamentalists, ironically, deny God when they assume the Bible is easy and that prayer is straightforward. But nor is prayer a mere act of self-reflection or even meditation, because that doesn't require a relationship with God. Prayer is a conduit, a bridge, between the Almighty and us. Yet neither is it totally rational, and no believer should try to argue otherwise. Only someone who misunderstands the nature of faith, God, spirituality, and prayer could argue that they're rational. Rational is easy; supernatural is much harder.

Søren Kierkegaard put it thus: "Just as in earthly life lovers long for the moment when they are able to breathe forth their love for each other, to let their souls blend in a soft whisper, so the mystic longs for the moment when in prayer he can, as it were, creep into God." Creeping into God. That's good, that's very good.

So, we're getting close to the end now. We've established that the rebel Christ didn't mention abortion, contraceptives, or assisted death, but he did expose and condemn hypocrisy, selfishness, and the dangers of wealth, anger, and inequality. He didn't speak of the free market, but he did reject those who transformed a place of worship into a market of profit. He didn't obsess about sex, but he did welcome and embrace those accused of sexual sin. He didn't build walls and fences, but he did insist that we rip down all that might separate and divide us. He didn't call for war and aggression, but did demand we throw away weapons and all that might hurt or kill our brothers and sisters. That is the rebel Christ: cutting through the pain and the suffering and the confusion of this broken planet and pulling back the curtain to show the splendid truth of the world's possibilities. He turns the world upside down, challenges the comfortable, sides with the outcast and the prisoner, has no regard for earthly power and worldly ambition. The rebellion of Christianity isn't safe and was never supposed to be. The rebellion of Christianity is dangerous.

Yet conservatives have transformed a faith that should revel in saying yes into a religion that cries no. Its founder died so that we would change the world, but many of his followers link Jesus to military force and dismiss those who campaign for social change as radical and even godless. So many conservatives have manipulated Christianity into a cult of the bunker, seeing persecution around every corner and retreating into literalism and small-mindedness. This is all nostalgia rather than the rebel Jesus. It's as though the cosmetics of the Gospel, the veneer of the message, have become more important than its core and its central meaning. Jesus spoke less about the end times than the time to end injustice, less about whom we should love than about how we should love everyone. The pain of another is personal pain, we are our neighbour, we exist and live in a collective of grace, and to exclude any other person is to exclude God. It's a message that should positively bleed from our very soul. We must extend the circle of love rather than stand at the corners of a square and repel outsiders. It was the rebel Christ who shaped Martin Luther King's struggle against racism, William Wilberforce's campaign against slavery, and Lord Ashley's work against child labour. It was the rebel Christ who led Dietrich Bonhoeffer to give his life to resisting Nazism.

Another of those personal stories. Only one more after this, I promise. The first time I visited Bethlehem, the place where the rebel Christ was born, I thought I was going to die. Leaving the town to re-enter Israel, I waited at the security checkpoint for the bored-looking, terrifyingly young soldier to check me through. In front of me was an elderly Palestinian man with his little grandson. There was a problem with their papers and the grandfather noisily tried to explain the situation. He then motioned to the child standing at his side, who proceeded to lift up his shirt to reveal a package clumsily taped to his belly. This was at the height of the time of suicide bombings, and all I could think was that this was such a surreal way and place to die. This was it, I was going to die.

The appendage was actually a colostomy bag, and the boy had an urgent appointment at an Israeli hospital. He was allowed through, and taken by a taxi to be cared for and looked after. In a virtual trance I showed my passport, was casually nodded through, and drove back to my hotel.

An hour later I sat in that Jerusalem hotel room and suddenly burst into tears. Not out of fear, I think, but out of despair. Salt-stained, sorrow-stained, and pain-stained despair. A despair that in Bethlehem, where I believe that the great conduit of grace came into this world, so much suffering and confusion could still breathe and flourish. Not only in Bethlehem, of course, but throughout the entire world; and the shadows of cruelty and suffering often appear not to be diminishing but positively growing in their clawing darkness.

How, then, can I still believe in a loving God and how can I be convinced that the rebel Christ is his son and that there is a greater and higher truth? How can I be convinced that love is the great power and that a baby born to a poor family in an occupied land two thousand years ago opened a door to eternal happiness and completion?

Sometimes it's grimly difficult, sometimes exuberantly compelling. But while my intensity of belief may vary, and while I often fail and fall, I haven't doubted the faith since accepting the Christian narrative more three decades ago. On a personal level, I'm convinced my relationship with Jesus became its most authentic only when I abandoned what was often religious pedantry for something far more progressive and vulnerable. I stopped speaking and started listening, entered into belief as a dialogue, opened my eyes rather than folded my arms. Yes, I met the rebel Christ.

He taught the liberation of the soul as well as of the person, and pleaded for a preferential option not just for the poor but also for the needy, the marginalized, the despised, and the oppressed. He also spoke of a preferential option for the Earth.

Yet so many of us in the Christian church have twisted the Messiah out of shape and out of recognition. We have perverted what are pristine teachings calling for radical action and a world shaped anew into stale conservatism. Too many of us have disguised the Jesus philosophy and painted it as a fetish of reactionary ideas around gender, sex, power, relationships, and personal choice.

Please believe me when I say that Jesus would not hurt or abuse, would not reject, would not exclude. He would not deny climate change, would not build walls, would not obsess about procreation, and would not condemn you for whom you loved. We live in an age of broken relationships and broken understanding, and the thread of humanity that could reattach us to the true rhythms of meaning and community is the rebel Christ whom we have often obscured. If there is a war on Christianity it's not fought by militant secularists but by Christians who prefer Christian talk to the Christian message. The baby who became a man who insisted we start a revolution of love, and who demanded that we join the rebellion that has no end.

Has the church, in whatever of its denomination forms, always acted justly? You know the answer as well as I do. Churches have betrayed Jesus just as individual Christians — including me — have betrayed him. There have been exceptions beyond counting, of course, but only a fanatic, and a myopic one at that, would try to make the case for a historically Christlike church. Matters are bad enough today, so we don't have to imagine too hard to realize what it must have been like when the church enjoyed state power. I could argue that lovers betray love, that democrats betray democracy, and people betray humanity, but that doesn't help. I've always found the statement that "religion causes all the wars" or that "more wars are fought in the name of religion than any other cause" too sweeping, in that it's not actually true, and that many of these conflicts — I've covered some in Ireland and the Middle East — are more about tribe than faith. But that won't help, either. The rebel Christ has simply not been reflected in the Christian world to anything like what was required, what was demanded. But there is still time, there is always time.

It would also be comforting to say that all of these errors, all of this misunderstanding, was in and of the past, but it's not true. We've seen in this book that it's not true. Every day as a cleric and as a journalist I'm stunned by the grace and goodness, but also the hatred and hysteria, of people who label themselves Christian.

I've used some personal stories throughout the book, and I'd like to end with another, perhaps the most important to me.

It's more than two decades ago. The telephone rings — it's a land line, and it makes a very traditional, even comforting noise. I lift the handset from the base, and the voice is that of my mum in London, England. Three thousand miles away, and back then you could almost hear the sound waves fighting against the distance. In spite of the cloudiness of the reception, I can tell that something is wrong. "Mum, what is it, what's happened?" "It's dad," she replies, "he's had a very bad stroke. They're not sure if he's going to pull through." I say that I'm on my way, and by eleven that evening I'm boarding a transatlantic flight.

The following morning I'm at Heathrow, then across London to my parents' small home in an eastern suburb. I hug my mum, I tell her that no, I don't want a cup of tea, then we drive my dad's used car to the local hospital, and there is Phil Coren. A tough, strong, and capable man. But it's as though he's become a child again. There he is in bed, in an ill-fitting gown, an intravenous drip in his arm, some stitches in his head from where he had fallen, his eyes glazed, his stare nowhere. The doctor tells us that it's not good but that there is so much about brain injury that they just don't know. Have faith. Yes, we have faith.

Frankly though, we don't know what to do. Mum talks about small things, I talk about small things. Then a big thing happens. The doors of the ward open and my sister comes in. Then my brother-in-law, then their eldest daughter. And, just like us, none of them know what to do. Five educated and worldly people who have absolutely no idea what to do, don't know how to help an adored man who is in a terrible condition. Then someone else comes in, and she knows exactly what to do. This is Katie, my sister's other, younger daughter. She storms into the room like a force of nature, a bolt of lightning.

Then, horror of horrors, she jumps on the bed. Then she puts her arms around her grandpa, and then she falls asleep. She does that because that's what she always does when she visits grandpa in the morning, when he's still in bed. No need to change now just because there are tubes and smells and noises.

And for the first time in thirty-six hours my father shows emotion, shows reaction. He cries. Tears begin to pour, bisecting his cheeks. Then, slowly, gradually his eyes seem to lose their milkiness, he seems to become alive and aware, and he turns his head. Toward me. We sit in silence, unsure, uncertain. Then Dad's lips begin to move, to tremble, and with an effort that must have been superhuman he begins to form a word. The word is my name. "Michael … Michael."

We press the panic button, the call button, and a doctor in a white coat is with us in moments. He checks, examines, thinks. Looks at Dad over and over again. Then turns to us with a broad smile and says, "This is amazing, this wasn't supposed to happen. It's like a miracle!" He didn't mean that this was in any way biblical, but that this wasn't in the medical textbook. But he was right. It was a miracle, it was the miracle of unconditional love. My dad had a remarkable, glorious recovery.

There's something I need to make clear about this story. That little girl wasn't, isn't like the rest of us. She's handicapped, disabled, challenged, use whatever word suits.

Katie is profoundly autistic. She's perhaps too trusting, too tactile in a way that some people find uncomfortable, she laughs and speaks when it might not be considered acceptable or "normal." She needs a lot of help, a lot of care, a lot of love. And in return she offers that help, that care, and that love. Unconditional love. On that day, that day of wonders, Katie offered and gave the gift of unconditional love. It changed a life, it changes lives, it changes the whole world. Unconditional love. Miraculous, extraordinary, life-changing, world-changing, unconditional love. That is the rebel Christ.

There we have it. In this brief, sometimes personal, sometimes analytical book I've tried to open a window just a little onto what I believe faith in the man who was Jesus who was God is supposed to be. It's supposed to be about him, about the rebel Christ. I pray, oh how I pray, that I have at least helped a little in this greatest of all struggles, in this vocation that I cherish every moment of my life. If not, please forgive me. Thing is, I know that he will. It's what he does. He's the rebel Christ.

Bibliography

I don't want to give an extensive bibliography, but rather just a list of a very few books that have been enormously helpful to me — and will, I hope, be to you as well. For each of these there are dozens more. Regarding the version of the Bible that I'd recommend, it's often a personal choice. My preference is for the New Revised Standard Version (NRSV), which is the one I've used in most of the book, but I'd also suggest looking at *The Message*, a modern and delightful translation by the late Eugene Peterson.

Borg, Marcus. *Days of Awe and Wonder: How to Be a Christian in the Twenty-First Century*. New York: HarperOne, 2017.

———. *The Heart of Christianity: Rediscovering a Life of Faith*. San Francisco: Harper San Francisco, 2003.

Boswell, John. *Same-Sex Unions in Premodern Europe*. New York: Villard, 1994.

Brueggemann, Walter. *Truth Speaks to Power: The Countercultural Nature of Scripture*. Louisville, KY: Westminster John Knox Press, 2013.

———. *An Unsettling God: The Heart of the Hebrew Bible*. Minneapolis: Augsburg Fortress, 2009.

Coles, Richard. *Bringing in the Sheaves: Wheat and Chaff from My*

Years as a Priest. London: Weidenfeld & Nicolson, 2016.
——. *Fathomless Riches: Or, How I Went From Pop to Pulpit*. London: Weidenfeld & Nicolson, 2014.
Fraser, Giles. *Chosen: Lost and Found Between Christianity and Judaism*. London: Allen Lane, 2021.
Helminiak, Daniel A. *What the Bible Really Says About Homosexuality*. Tajique, NM: Alamo Square, 1994.
John, Jeffrey. *Permanent, Faithful, Stable: Christian Same-Sex Marriage*. London: Darton, Longman & Todd, 1993.
MacCulloch, Diarmaid. *A History of Christianity: The First Three Thousand Years*. London: Allen Lane, 2009.
——. *Reformation: Europe's House Divided, 1490–1700*. London: Allen Lane, 2003.
Oakley, Mark. *The Collage of God*. London: Darton, Longman & Todd, 2001.
——. *The Splash of Words*. London: Canterbury Press Norwich, 2016.
Sacks, Jonathan. *Morality: Restoring the Common Good in Divided Times*. New York: Basic Books, 2020.
——. *Not in God's Name: Confronting Religious Violence*. Toronto: Random House, 2015.
Wallis, Jim. *Christ in Crisis: Why We Need to Reclaim Jesus*. New York: HarperCollins, 2019.
Williams, Rowan. *Being Christian: Baptism, Bible, Eucharist, Prayer*. Grand Rapids, MI: Eerdmans, 2014.
——. *Being Human: Bodies, Minds, Persons*. Grand Rapids, MI: Eerdmans, 2016.
——. *The Way of St. Benedict*. New York: Bloomsbury Continuum, 2020.
Wilson, Alan. *More Perfect Union?: Understanding Same-Sex Marriage*. London: Darton, Longman & Todd, 2014.
Wright, N.T. *Interpreting Jesus: Essays on the Gospels*. Grand Rapids, MI: Zondervan, 2020.
——. *Paul: A Biography*. San Francisco: HarperOne, 2018.

About the Author

MICHAEL COREN is a broadcaster, columnist, and speaker. He hosted a daily television show for fifteen years for which he won numerous awards. Michael is a columnist for the *Toronto Star* and a frequent contributor to the *Globe and Mail* and other Canadian and British publications. He is the bestselling author of seventeen books, including biographies of G.K. Chesterton, H.G. Wells, Arthur Conan Doyle, J.R.R. Tolkien, and C.S. Lewis, and has contributed to the *Dictionary of National Biography* and several other anthologies. Michael has published in many countries and in more than a dozen languages. In 2005, he won the Edward R. Murrow Award for Radio Broadcasting; in 2006, the RTDNA Canada Radio Broadcasting Award; in 2007, the Communicator Award in Hollywood; and in 2008, the Omni Award for his television show. In 2012, he was awarded the Queen's Jubilee Medal for services to media. Michael is ordained in the Anglican Church of Canada.